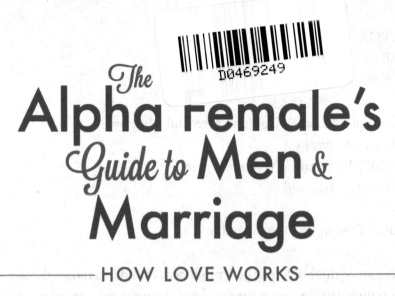

The Alpha Female's Guide to Men & Marriage

HOW LOVE WORKS

SUZANNE VENKER

A POST HILL PRESS BOOK
ISBN: 978-1-61868-844-6
ISBN (eBook): 978-1-61868-845-3

The Alpha Female's Guide to Men and Marriage:
How Love Works
© 2017 by Suzanne Venker
All Rights Reserved

Cover Design by Quincy Avilio

Post Hill Press
posthillpress.com

Published in the United States of America

For Bill,
my best decision to date.

It is part of maturity to realize you might have been walking up the wrong road and to be willing to try a new road.

—Susan Page

CONTENTS

CONTENTS

A NOTE FROM THE AUTHOR

The book you're holding (or reading online) is not yet another manual written by a psychologist about how to make your marriage work. It is somewhat about the latter, but it is so much more. It's not an easy book to read, either. You have to be both self-reflective and independent minded to absorb it, otherwise you run the risk of becoming defensive or angry. Or both. That's because it asks a lot of you.

I am a cultural critic. Over the past fifteen years, I've read literally hundreds of books, newspaper and magazine articles, scholarly papers, and blog posts on marriage and relationships, on work-family conflict, and on feminism and gender politics. I've attended conferences, given speeches, and written extensively (five books in total) about these issues and as a result have received scores of emails from men and women across the country and beyond.

I don't claim to know everything, but this much I do know: the culture in which you live is designed to make you fail as a wife. *The Alpha Female's Guide to Men and Marriage* is the cure you need to thwart such influences and to find peace with a man. The book is, at its core, about how love works and about why so many women aren't privy to this information—or if they are, why they reject it.

It's also about my own story. I married for the first time at 23 and for the second at 30. My first marriage lasted four years and produced no children. My second husband and I have been married 18 years, and we have a daughter and a son who are now in their teens. That I've been a wife for more than two decades doesn't mean I've always been a good one. For I am, dear readers, an alpha female like you. The reasons I am may differ from yours, but the end result is the same.

I had to learn the hard way how to love a man.

Alpha females aren't new, but they were once a rare breed. They were the women in our mothers' day who didn't follow conventional paths. They became writers and politicians, or actresses and scientists, or doctors and artists. Or they *were* traditional housewives but went into "mother mode" and never came out. Their husbands became one more child to lead and instruct—which no man wants. As a friend of mine, a married dentist and father of three, told me, "The world needs alpha females, but I don't."

An alpha female is, above all else, a leader. As a wife, you may find her at the office or you may find her at home with the kids. How the alpha wife spends her days doesn't matter—what matters is how she behaves. The alpha wife takes charge of everything and everyone. She is, in a word, The Boss.

Problem is, no man wants a boss, or even a competitor, at home. That type of relationship may work for a spell, but it will eventually come crashing down. *The Alpha Female's Guide to Men and Marriage* is for women who don't want this to happen to them.

DISCLAIMERS

1. *The Alpha Female's Guide to Men and Marriage* is not for the woman whose husband has an addiction, or a mental illness, or who's abusive in any way. It is for women whose husbands are healthy, sober, and safe.

2. Despite the book's focus on wives, the advice herein applies to any woman who's in a long-term, monogamous relationship with a man.

3. *The Alpha Female's Guide to Men and Marriage* is about the needs and behaviors of men and women in general. There are always exceptions, but there's still a rule. This book is about the rule.

QUIZ: ARE YOU AN ALPHA WIFE?

Answer the questions below to find out if you're an alpha wife. Note: This quiz will only work if you're 100% honest in your answers.

1. Do you feel nervous or out of control when you're not the one in charge?

2. Are you a perfectionist or an overachiever?

3. Do you sometimes feel superior to your husband, as though he needs you to show him how to do things? (How to dress, what to say, how to grocery shop, how to parent, and so forth.)

4. Do you take your everyday frustrations out on your husband as though he's the cause of those frustrations?

5. Do you generally expect your husband to go along with your plans, as opposed to the other way around?

6. Do you listen to your husband when he has something to say without immediately formulating a response in your head?

7. Do you roll your eyes when your husband says something with which you disagree or disapprove?

8. Do you frequently contradict your husband? (If your answer is no, would your husband agree?)

9. Are you a drill sergeant?

10. Do you tease your husband in front of others in a manner that could be construed as disrespectful?

11. Do you need to be right?

12. Do you frequently interrupt your husband or talk over him, even in public? (If your answer is no, would your husband agree?)

13. Does your marriage feel like one giant power struggle? (If your answer is no, would your husband agree?)

Note: If you answered "yes" to three or more questions, you are indeed an alpha wife. But not every woman is the same degree of alpha. A good gauge of how alpha you are is simple: The more questions you answered in the affirmative, and the more frequently they each occur, the more alpha you are.

INTRODUCTION:
A NEW SET OF TOOLS

Would you like to dance?
Okay, but I have to warn you I tend to lead.
Of course. You're American.
— *Unfaithful*

This is the book I wish my mother had had. I think she might have wished that too.

Like me, my mother was not a perfect wife. She was, however, a remarkable and compassionate woman. And she was fiercely devoted to my father, so much so that five years after he died she couldn't bring herself to even kiss the man who fell in love with her at the independent living facility where she lived for a year and a half before she too passed away. The man wanted to marry her, but it was out of the question. In my mother's mind, there was only one man for her. That he was gone and she was technically available was beside the point.

Despite my mother's allegiance to my father, she never quite mastered wifedom for one reason—she was wholly unyielding. Fortunately, my father understood my mother in a way no one else did. Unfortunately, I think my mother took advantage of this fact. Not in a calculated or malicious way; I think she just got comfortable. My mother knew my father would never leave her. He'd already been divorced once and that had been a nightmare.

Plus, my parents had a great deal in common, and their priorities were perfectly aligned. They were married 44 years.

The problem, really, was that my father got what he wished for. His first wife had been a committed Catholic who didn't believe in birth control, not even of the natural variety. She was a follower, someone who did what The Church told her she ought to do— which was common among some Catholics in those days, at least in my neck of the woods. But after four children, my father made it clear to his then-wife he did not want more kids. Naturally, this put him in a quandary. He was only in his thirties, and already the sex was gone.

Enter my mother, who was, for the times at least, a liberated woman. She and my father met at Washington University in St. Louis, where my mother was taking my father's accounting class. He was a CPA, not a professor, but taught evening classes in accounting. (As it happens, both my parents graduated from Washington University, although they were seven years apart so they would not have met.) My mother had just returned to St. Louis from the East Coast, where she had received an MBA from Radcliffe and then worked in New York and Washington D.C. She decided to return home when her father became ill and resumed her career as a stockbroker.

My mother was what folks called then a "working girl"— with her very own apartment, no less. "I might as well have been a woman of the streets!" she used to say. She wasn't religious, either. My mother was raised Catholic but for a variety of reasons denounced her faith in her early twenties, which I suspect appealed to my Presbyterian father who'd had it up to here with Catholicism.

Given the precarious situation in which he found himself, it makes perfect sense that my father would fall head over heels.

He was vulnerable, to say the least, and because he didn't wear a wedding ring my mother didn't know he was married at first. So that's how their relationship began.

Not a good start, to be sure. But it would be difficult for any man in my father's circumstances to ignore my mother. She was a strong and beautiful woman with a fierce mind of her own, and she always had male admirers with whom she adored flirting. Unfortunately for them, that's just about all she did. My father was the one and only man to ever wear her down.

That's how my mother would talk to me about sex. "You have to be strong because men will try and wear you down," she'd say—emphasis on the phrase, "wear you down." Her beliefs about sex were dated but practical. My mother understood desire, but the idea that a woman would sleep with a man she didn't love or wasn't engaged to was repugnant. She was also extremely prudent, so the idea of not using birth control once married was nothing short of obtuse. This is in part what led to her break from Catholicism. Some of its tenets appealed to her—my mother was pro-marriage and pro-family—but most did not.

I'm not sure at what point my father wore my mother down; but they ultimately married in 1964, after years of being together while my father was getting a divorce from his first wife. In those days, it took more than irreconcilable differences to end a marriage. If one spouse didn't want the divorce—and my father's ex didn't—it could take years for the marriage to officially end, even if the couple is no longer living together. Even if one spouse is physically and emotionally unstable, which my father's ex was. At one point during their marriage, she kicked him in the groin after they had sex when he tried to avoid procreation. He lost one testicle.

Needless to say, my mother became embroiled in what was viewed as a scandal among family and friends. What people weren't privy to was the reality of my father's first marriage. My father was a good, kind and yes, even loyal man. But he was also a human being, and the marital predicament in which he found himself—which today would have a name—must have tugged at my mother's heartstrings and made her love him all the more. Indeed, she waited years before she and my father were finally able to marry; and I suspect my father was enormously humbled.

Whether or not my parents discussed having kids prior to getting married I honestly don't know, but I'm pretty sure my father assumed my mother didn't want children. Either that or he was so smitten he didn't care one way or the other. But since my mother was a 34-year-old, never-married career girl when they tied the knot—which at the time made her a virtual old maid—it would have been a fair assumption on his part to assume my mother wasn't maternal. But alas, my mother did want children, and out of four pregnancies altogether, she got two: my sister and me.

After my sister was born, my mother did something even more preposterous in those days: she went back to work! The story of her education and career track was profiled in the *St. Louis Post Dispatch*, circa 1966. Underneath the heading "Today's Women," the article highlighted my mother's choice to enter the field of investment banking (at a time when there were only three female stockbrokers in St. Louis), as well as her decision to return to work after the birth of her first child.

> My father loved my mother's unconventional ways and her ability to forge her own path. But he couldn't have anticipated how challenging, how maddening really, it would be to be married to her. Today there are millions of men like my father.

That last plan didn't work out too well. In fact, my mother "retired" from her 15-year career when my sister and I were 5 and 3, respectively. "Motherhood is a full time job," she'd say more than once as I was growing up. "You can't do both at once and do them well." (Talk about ahead of her time!)

As it happens, my mother remained unemployed from that point on. I think she'd planned to return to work at some point but over the years became involved in other pursuits—community gardening and historical preservation, to name a few—that would ultimately come to define her life.

To be sure, my mother's choice to postpone marriage and focus on a career instead was unusual for the times. She liked to say she "did things backwards." In her day, it was far more common to make the shift from wife and mother to working woman, if the shift occurred at all, than it was to transition from career girl to wife.

My mother, you see, was the quintessential alpha female.

An alpha female is capable, confident, ambitious and, above all, in charge. But not every alpha female is the same degree of alpha. As with all behavior, there's a spectrum. On a 10-point scale, an alpha female might be an 8 or a 5, or a 10 or a 3. (Because of this, not everything in this book will necessarily apply to you.) Still, most alphas have a certain disposition or temperament, a manner in which they're likely to act in most circumstances.

One thing *all* alphas are is difficult. With my mother, everything was a fight. Everything was "No" unless she determined it was appropriate to say "Yes." If my mother wasn't the one who made the decision, the decision couldn't possibly be good. Every so often she would appear to cede to my father's wishes, but only if she happened to agree with him.

You can imagine how well this went over with my father. He wanted a woman with her own mind, but he didn't know it would translate to so much conflict! He didn't know my mother's will would overpower his at every turn. That's what I meant when I said he got what he wished for. My father loved my mother's unconventional ways and her ability to forge her own path. But he couldn't have anticipated how challenging, how maddening really, it would be to be married to her.

Today there are millions of men like my father. The average woman today is just like my mother was: strong and independent, yet proud and dictatorial.

Fortunately, in my mother's case, her difficult ways were offset by her endearing personality. If I had to rate her level of alpha-ness, I'd give her an 8. She was capable of exhibiting very unpleasant behaviors, but she was also naturally forgiving and more gracious than anyone I've ever known. As a teenager, if I complained to my mother about someone I didn't like, she would never take my side. She refused to speak ill of anyone, even if the person deserved it. At the time I was frustrated by that; but in retrospect, it was incredibly admirable.

My mother was also fun and even hip for her day. Compared to her contemporaries, she was downright liberal—which was evident given her choice of friends, many of whom beat to a different drum. My mother was solidly conservative in her politics and demeanor; but she was sympathetic toward human nature, which made her far more humane than some of her contemporaries and family members.

Honestly, my mother's one and only flaw was her inability to cede control. But, that is no small thing. Controlling women are a challenge to live with, and they're usually critical to boot. While "critical" is not generally considered a positive trait, there are times when it can work in one's favor. People who have a critical eye are looking to improve things and thus have the ability to turn something mediocre into something fabulous (think Martha Stewart). But finding fault in a company is different from finding fault in the person you love.

If you took the alpha wife quiz and determined you're an alpha, I have some news that at first will be hard to swallow: you're going to have to cede control. If you don't, your marriage or relationship will continue to be one giant fight.

I know the idea of ceding control is daunting, especially today. The implication is that a wife who yields to her husband in any way invariably loses her identity. Doing so means he'll lord over her. (Hint: he won't.) To avoid this supposed fate, women are taught to chuck their femininity and to become more like men: dominant, aggressive, and in charge.

That may get you ahead at work. But at home, it will land you in a ditch.

Former Fox News anchor E.D. Hill is a great example of the modern woman's conundrum. In *Going Places: How America's Best and Brightest Got Started Down the Road of Life*, Hill talks of being raised by a mother who taught her to learn to do everything herself—even the typically male tasks. "Be able to stand on your own," her mother told her.

Millions of women heard a similar refrain from their mothers growing up. (For the record, I did not.) And while it's good to be self-sufficient, particularly when you're single, insisting that a woman doesn't need a man is a terrible precedent for marriage.

"There is a downside to being so self-reliant," writes Hill. "I found it very difficult to let anyone help me. And if they tried but couldn't do it as well I could, I was disappointed. That often left me frustrated ... I couldn't stop myself from proving that I didn't need [my husband] to do things for me. Needless to say, this "power struggle," along with other issues, put a big strain on our relationship, and he is now my ex."[1]

Thanks to feminism, this 'power struggle' Hill describes is par for the course. Women today are effectively at war with the men in their lives, sometimes unknowingly. Even women who don't consider themselves feminist have a feminist mind and as a result don't understand men and marriage. The idea that the sexes are "equal," as in *the same,* has supplanted what past generations have always known: that men and women are vastly different creatures. And that dismissing these differences makes marriage hell.

My mother was fortunate not to have been raised in such an environment. She knew a very different America, one that honored men and marriage. She certainly wasn't raised to think she didn't need a man! A product of the Depression, my mother would never have said or even felt such a thing, even if her behavior implied otherwise. The only reason her behavior *did* imply otherwise is because my mother didn't trust a soul. And people who lack the ability to trust compensate by taking control.

> While it's good to be self-sufficient, insisting that a woman doesn't need a man is a terrible precedent for a marriage.

Here's a great example. In the film *Leap Year*, the main character Anna (played by Amy Adams) is the ultimate alpha female. Toward the end of the film, Declan, Anna's love interest, says to her, "Why don't you stop trying to control everything in the known universe? It's dinner. Have a little faith that it will all work out."[2]

To which Anna replies, "I've heard that one before." Then she launches into the reason why she's the way she is because her father couldn't hold a job, which led to constant financial instability—including her family home getting repossessed. When Declan responds to this information with genuine surprise and compassion, one detects in Anna a moment of vulnerability. But then she resumes her controlling ways.

There are so many reasons why women become alphas. Maybe you're a product of divorce and don't trust love. Maybe your father was a cad, and you don't trust men. Maybe your mother ruled the roost, and you've never had any other model. Or maybe, like Anna, you grew up in a home where there was never enough money and you therefore became determined to make your own way. Conversely, maybe you grew up privileged. This can also make a woman an alpha. Alphas are rarely satisfied, which makes it impossible for a man to please her.

But most women become alphas due to a simple lack of trust. It isn't always directed toward men—it may just be an inability to trust in general. But at the end of the day, it doesn't matter why a woman develops a tough exterior. The root of the problem is the same: fear. Women who insist on being The Boss are afraid if they let down their guard, they'll get hurt. Either that or they won't get what they want.

While the scenarios above can occur in an era, it was 1960s feminism that drove the nail in the coffin. It taught women that society (read: men) has oppressed them, and that the only way for a woman to be empowered is to become fiercely independent and to hurl demands on men and society. A woman should put herself first at all times and never, *ever* cede control. The result is a generation of women who believe they don't need a man at all.

That attitude will destroy your marriage before you return from the honeymoon.

I honestly believe what women struggle with is this: Can a woman be strong, yet still be vulnerable and even take care of a husband? Can she be a wife and still maintain her own identity? Is it possible to be powerful outside the home, yet defer to a husband inside the home? Yes, yes, and yes.

But first you'll have to Let Go. Of your desire to lead. Of your desire to be in control. And of your desire to have the last word.

Then you'll need a new set of tools. Work is about making money or having power and influence—marriage is about love. If you want to be successful in both arenas, you'll need to be able to switch gears. You need to take off your "I'm in charge" hat and surrender to love at home. (This holds true whether you're the boss at work or the boss of your kids.) The reason so many successful career women are single or divorced is because they never mastered this delicate balance. And mothers at home are just as susceptible to becoming alpha wives since that role is a position of leadership too.

I know what I'm proposing is no small thing. It requires a huge mental shift, and you will get little, if any, support from the culture.

The folks in your midst will insist you shouldn't have to "change a damn thing" for your husband. After all, the woman you are at work is your real self, and why should you hide your real self from your husband? If he can't handle a powerful woman, he must be weak. "A real man can handle a strong woman," they'll say.

> Your husband is responsible for his own actions, but his behavior is inextricably linked to yours. That is the secret of the male-female dance.

I agree a real man can handle a strong woman. In fact, many men prefer strong women—*if* by strong we mean a woman who's confident, who knows herself, and who can hold her own in a conversation. But a strong-*willed* woman who has to have her way all the time isn't enticing in the least. Neither is the liberated woman who carries her empowered self with her like an appendage, as though she doesn't need a man at all. Such women end up in a war with husbands who are simply trying to love them.

The way to avoid this is to own your feminine.

The Alpha Female's Guide to Men and Marriage is about learning to let go of the wheel. It's about learning to love your husband in a whole new way in order to bring about a more peaceful union. If you want to be happily married, you must relinquish the desire to be right. "Being right is a dead end," writes relationship expert Susan Page. "Life just stops there. Nothing else happens...."

For the record, I realize your husband has areas in which he, too, can improve. But you can't browbeat your husband into becoming who you want him to become. Your husband is responsible for his own behavior, but his behavior is inextricably linked to yours. That is the secret of the male-female dance.

A woman's love, along with her femininity, can reduce the most powerful man in the world to mere jellyfish. Your husband, whether he's a CEO or a handyman, wants to make you happy more than anything else in the world. It's what he lives for.

If this isn't the husband you know, it's possible you're not responding to him in a kind and loving manner. It's possible you're not taking care of his needs the way you expect him to take care of yours. It's possible you're not letting him know you respect him and that you're grateful to have him in your life.

"But what if I genuinely don't feel that way about my husband?" you ask. If you feel absolutely nothing for your husband—zero admiration, respect, or desire—I admit that's a problem. But it's probably not the case. More than likely, you do feel this way about him but forgot you do because of conflicts that have surfaced along the way. After all, you felt this way about him when you married him. Didn't you?

If so, you have the power to change your marriage overnight. Boom—just like that. Women have a natural feminine energy that, when used well, works wonders on men and marriage. Too many women give up on love before putting this power to use. And it's just sitting there for the taking! Not using it is like flushing a million dollars down the toilet. So before you make another move, look in the mirror and ask yourself what *you* bring to the marriage table. Because the tenor of your home is a direct result of the energy you bring forth.

What kind of energy are you supplying?

1

WAVE THE WHITE FLAG

It was the A.1. Sauce that did it. I was cleaning up the last of the table items in our dining room after dinner, and I noticed a bottle of A.1. Sauce on the floor next to my husband's chair. Naturally, I thought that was an odd place for it to be, so I went into the kitchen where my husband was doing the dishes and asked him what the A.1. Sauce was doing on the floor. "You never like it when I use sauce on my food," he said.

It was at that moment when I realized what kind of wife I'd become: the kind who micromanages every move her husband makes, so much so he has to hide a bottle of sauce on the floor so he can eat his damn dinner in peace.

My husband called it "directing his traffic." That's a polite way of saying I tell him what to do, how to do it, and when to do it. No husband wants a wife like that, but mine was particularly insistent. A product of divorce and the youngest of six (the next sibling being seven years older than he), my husband spent a lot of time alone as a child and as a result became fiercely independent. He's also a man, and at the time I didn't understand the scope of what that meant. All I knew was I could not tell my husband anything—what to do, what to say, what to wear—and I had no choice but to accept it.

Which was hard because I come from a long line of alpha females, so instructing people is in my blood. When I was young and would play with my friends, for example, I was always the leader. There was no discussion about it; I'd just announce it outright. Fortunately, I was never mean or nasty about it and as a result had plenty of friends. I suppose that's why I never thought of this trait as a negative quality, per se. I got things done! I made things happen!

I remember my mentor in high school wrote a college recommendation on my behalf and referred to me as "a born leader." That was one of the reasons I became a teacher. Then later I became a mother, and of course that job involves *a lot* of traffic directing. So it was only natural I'd begin instructing my husband as well. Plus that was the model I'd had as a child.

As for the A.1. Sauce, I'd been on my husband for years about his eating habits and considered it my job to educate him about how to be healthy, just as I do with our kids. When I first met my husband, he was going to the gym every morning at 5:30 am. He was also 40 pounds lighter. But after years of harping on him with no results, I couldn't shake the feeling it was my fault he wasn't taking care of himself.

> A man's reaction to being told what to do by his wife is to do the exact opposite.

Naturally, I didn't see it that way at first. Why is it *my* fault if my husband makes bad choices? He's lucky to have me guiding him! I'm just being helpful! But what controlling wives call helpful, husbands call something else. A man's reaction to being told what to do by his wife is to do the exact opposite. Indeed, it wasn't until I *stopped* getting on my husband's case that he began to take better care of himself.

Huh—go figure.

My light bulb moment didn't end there. Once I saw the connection between the two—my dictating and my husband's lack of motivation—I started thinking about other ways I was behaving that would cause him to react negatively. Like the times I'd tell him how to drive, or I'd correct his language, or I'd complain about whatever he wasn't doing well and how he could improve.

Then one night I saw myself in Ken Burns' documentary *The Roosevelts: An Intimate History.* The narrator said this about Franklin in reference to his wife Eleanor: "He wanted someone who had all the devotion to him that his mother had had but not the admonitory part—the part that told him what to do and what not to do. And sadly, Eleanor couldn't be worshipful and had to be admonitory."[1]

Eureka.

My mother was an Eleanor Roosevelt.

So was I.

I know the idea of being "worshipful" toward your husband sounds extreme, and perhaps it is. But men hate to be told what to do, and they adore praise. So really, there's no way around it. If you want a peaceful marriage, you have to be the antithesis of Eleanor Roosevelt. You have to stop dictating and start doting instead.

You must also abdicate your impulse to lead. Most marital conflicts amount to a simple power struggle: two people are trying to drive the same car. And that doesn't work. The only way to put an end to the struggle is for one partner to capitulate, or to sit in the passenger seat. Not the back seat—the passenger seat. (That's an important distinction.) And for many sound reasons, all of which I hope will be clear by the time you finish this book, I'm suggesting that person be you.

Alphas and Betas

In the past, alpha females such as Eleanor Roosevelt (and my mother) were a rarer breed. Today they are commonplace. The words "alpha" and "beta" refer to a personality type and are sometimes referred to as type A and type B. Alphas, or type As, are very ambitious. They typically can't rest until they've achieved a task, whatever it may be. They're doers, not talkers. They can also become impatient with delays and with a lack of efficiency or productivity. They can lose their temper easily. On the upside, alphas are generally successful at whatever they do—not because they're smarter or better than anyone else but because they persevere where others give up.

Betas, or type Bs, are more laid back. They're patient, easygoing, and rarely in a hurry. Known as socializers, these individuals are slower to move and tend to talk about doings things as opposed to actually doing them. They also procrastinate. These traits are very frustrating for the alpha, who's prone to action.

At the same time, there are moments when sitting back and letting life happen, as opposed to forcing everything into a box, can be advantageous. Indeed, where the beta is careful and calculating, the alpha can be impulsive.

Both traits, in other words, have their strengths and weaknesses.

If I had to choose the main difference between alphas and betas, it's that alphas almost always speak their mind while betas do not. To be sure, speaking one's mind is important. But sometimes not speaking one's mind is just as powerful. This is something betas understand intuitively. Since Americans tend to value those who speak up more than they do those who are quiet, alphas tend to garner more respect than betas. That is to our discredit, since the beta offers a wealth of wisdom. The alpha just has to be quiet long enough to hear what the beta has to say.

Two great ways to tell whether a person is an alpha or a beta is by the way he or she drives a car and the way he or she behaves in a restaurant. The road is a great metaphor for determining one's personality type. Alphas tend to anticipate rather than react. If they see a long line in an exit lane, for instance, they might not get in the back of the line and wait patiently with the others but will instead drive in the adjacent lane and when they see an opening closer to the exit, move into line. Obnoxious and unfair? Yes, but alphas are myopic about getting where they need to go.

Betas, as a rule, are more relaxed behind the wheel and are therefore more generous with their fellow drivers. They'll watch people get upset behind the wheel and find it fascinating, or they may mumble to themselves about how stupid the other driver is. But they won't react with outward aggression.

At restaurants, the alpha is the person who demands good service, while the beta doesn't make a fuss. This scenario is a great example of how both personalities are equally flawed. On the one hand, people should expect good food and service for a meal they're paying for and should speak up if it the food isn't to their satisfaction—which can be done in either a rude or a polite manner.

Conversely, betas believe it's important not to let the money spent or the quality of the food and service override the experience of spending time with someone you care about. Because of this, they're more likely to accept an unsatisfactory meal than they are to complain about it.

Now there's an important caveat to all of this: most people are neither 100% beta nor 100% alpha. Someone who's 100% beta is someone who has no opinions (or who never shares them), no identity, and very little self-esteem. This person does not value his or her needs at all. Someone who's 100% alpha, on the other hand, is, well, a bitch or an ass. This person appears to have an inflated ego but in reality is likely insecure. Her or she has a hard time incorporating other people's needs into the equation. We all run into folks like this on occasion; but they're the exception, not the rule.

Most of us are some combination of alpha and beta, though we typically lean to one side. The problem women have today is they've been conditioned to bury their beta-like ways and to assert themselves at all times in a masculine, or alpha-like, manner. The result is that we're drowning in alphas. We're inbreeding! And that doesn't work. Every alpha needs a beta, and every beta needs an alpha. Getting the balance right can be tricky, but it is vital for your marriage that you do.

To get an idea of where you fall on the spectrum, I suggest taking the online alpha/beta quiz by psychotherapist Dr. Sonya Rhodes, author of *The Alpha Woman Meets Her Match*. While I don't agree at all with Rhodes' analysis of gender relations—she has nothing but praise for the alpha female—the quiz itself is very good. Respondents are asked to put a check mark next to the phrases that best describe him or her. Here's a sampling:

☐ I tend to be bossy.

☐ I try hard to please my partner.

☐ People sometimes say I'm arrogant.

☐ I try to see other points of view.

☐ I procrastinate on projects at work and at home.

☐ I can crush people with my criticism.

☐ I'm a doer, not a talker.

☐ I am super confident.

☐ I frequently lie awake at night thinking about what I should have said.

☐ It's better to be gentle than blunt.

☐ I tend to be a laid back person.

☐ I make decisions quickly. Why waste time?

☐ I try to please people a lot.

☐ I empathize easily with other people's problems.

☐ Once I make up my mind, I'm hard to budge.

After you take the quiz, you'll get a score that reads like this: "high alpha/low beta," "high beta/low alpha," "high alpha/mid beta," and so forth. (Each result has a color as an identifier.) Keep in mind that not every person will fit the mold perfectly. A beta, for example, can still be competitive or opinionated despite his or her easy-going manner. And an alpha can be a genuinely nice person.

But wherever you fall on the spectrum, the quiz should give you a good idea of how alpha or beta you are.

When I took the quiz, I landed in the yellow box—which means I'm "high alpha/mid beta." That makes sense, since true alphas (those in the red zone) are "exceedingly dominant" and "downright bossy," which is not a fair depiction of me. A true alpha female would never question her alpha-like ways, much less believe in toning them down. A true alpha female is proud and defensive of her dictatorial style and has difficulty looking in the mirror. She can also be mean.

There's a natural synergy to a marriage when the man is more dominant than the woman. When it's reversed, it feels off.

As a mid-beta, I'm someone who's willing to yield for the sake of peace. If I were a high alpha/low beta, it would be much harder to do this. Here's the description of my personality profile:

You are High Alpha and Mid Beta, which means you are dominant in most relationships but have the capacity to collaborate and compromise. However, you have to guard against imposing your strong will and overpowering people. You will match up well with a partner who has a strong Mid to High Beta profile and will allow your Alpha to lead. Your best match is with someone more laid back than you, who will help you take the edge off when necessary.

Imposing your strong will. Now that describes me to a T—and my mother, and my grandmother, and my great-grandmother, and my aunt, and, well, just about every woman on my mother's side of the family. Whenever I meet women who are not like this—women who are softer, quieter and more gentle than I—I feel a twinge of envy because their lives and their relationships seem so much calmer in comparison.

Sadly, American culture no longer reveres the beta female prototype. But in my experience, beta females are happier and more relaxed, not to mention easier to get along with. They also don't struggle as much in their relationships with men—there's a natural synergy to a marriage when the man is more dominant than the woman. When it's reversed, it feels off. There's friction where there should be peace.

After you take the quiz, you'll probably discover you and your husband are a mix of alpha and beta. That's good. What you don't want is for each of you to be strongly in one camp. When two alphas get together, it's combustible! When two betas get together, nothing gets done. The goal is to have symmetry.

If you do determine you're an alpha, and you probably are since you're reading this book, you might think it isn't possible to change your ways even if you agree you should. I used to think that. I thought that whatever one's natural propensities were was something my husband would just have to accept. In other words, since I have an alpha personality, and my husband chose me, obviously he must like that about me so he's just going to have to live with it!

But just because we're inclined toward a specific way of behaving doesn't mean we're powerless over it. You can change your behavior anytime you want.

Changing the Brain

It all starts in the brain. Brain research has exploded in recent years, and what experts have learned is that we can train our brains to think the way we want them to. One great way to do this is to repeat a mantra over and over again, hundreds or even thousands of times per day.

I know that sounds daunting, but stay with me. Let's say you want to slow down more and not move so fast. So you come up with a short, easy phrase that represents the change you want to make—such as, "I choose to slow down"—and you repeat that phrase every chance you get throughout the day.

You can say it while you're driving in a car or when you're in the bathroom. You can say it when you're doing the dishes, taking a walk, or waiting in line. On any given day, there are a myriad of opportunities to repeat a simple phrase in your head. Over time, your brain will reset itself. In this case, slowing down will become more natural.

It's all about forming new habits. The research says it's extremely difficult to get rid of a bad habit. But if you develop a new habit, it will eventually replace the old one. So for instance if you want to drink less, it won't work if you just tell yourself you're going to drink less. You have to *do* something specific to change your behavior, such as take a bath or a walk or do your errands at the time you would normally pour a glass of wine. You have to replace the old habit with a new one.

To be less controlling, then, you might say to yourself "I choose to say nothing" when your husband says something with which you disagree. Choose the behavior you think has the most potential for conflict and talk yourself into doing the opposite of that behavior by creating a mantra that pushes you in that direction.

There are so many ways I used to be controlling, though I never thought of it as such. When I would talk on my husband's behalf, for instance, I was just trying to help him be clearer with his message since he has a tendency to ramble. He'll start off great, but sometimes he veers down a different path and winds up in a ditch. When he's finished talking, people will get a look on their face that says, "What did he just say?" I would especially chime in if he'd had too much to drink because then it gets really bad.

But imagine if someone talked on your behalf. Even if you knew you had a tendency to ramble, you wouldn't want someone to point it out. While I was trying to help my husband get his point across, and may have been successful in doing so, I was also creating a rift between us. He would chalk those instances up as disrespect and hold that feeling inside. Then it would emerge later, usually in some random fashion, and I'd be stuck trying to put the pieces of the puzzle together.

In a futile attempt to stop my behavior, I'd let my husband know in a different way that he wasn't making sense. If his story started to go south, I'd give him The Look. The poor man got so used to The Look that even when I eventually stopped, I'd notice his eyes turn toward me in anticipation of The Look—which was hardly an improvement. "You can tell people they are wrong by a look or an intonation or a gesture just as eloquently as you can in words," wrote Dale Carnegie in *How to Win Friends and Influence People*.[2]

One thing I don't do, but I see a lot of wives do, is identify their husbands' shortcomings in public. They'll point something out they know their husbands feel insecure about—say he's short, or he doesn't make as much money as he'd like, or he has a nervous tick. (My husband feels inadequate about not being handy.) Never point out your husband's Achilles heel in the company of others. If you do, it will come back to bite you in the ass. Besides, it's mean.

All of this is to say: don't do what I did. Don't wait for an A.1. Sauce moment to change. Ask yourself now if your marriage feels competitive rather than complementary. If you find yourself beating your head against the wall, trying to get your husband to see things your way and he won't, that's when you know it's time for a change.

Only it isn't your husband who needs to change. It's you.

I know this is hard to accept. I know it doesn't seem fair. But that's only because you're approaching your problems in a manner over which you have no control. You cannot change anyone, least of all your husband, by browbeating him into what you want him to be. Telling your husband he's wrong in an effort to get him to change will only make him dig his heels in all the more. It will never, *ever* make him change. (More on this in Chapter 6.) Which means the only option you have as a wife, the only genuine control you have to improve your relationship, is to change yourself. Change the way you approach the issue, and you will get a different result.

With that in mind, commit yourself—right now, today—to being a different kind of wife. It's not something that will happen overnight; but hour by hour, day by day, week by week, month by month, year by year, you will learn how powerful, how *liberating*, it is to wave the white flag. To cede control. Remember what I wrote in the introduction: at the heart of your need to control is fear, or an inability to trust. You must learn to trust if you're going to establish a better relationship with your husband. There's no other way.

To be sure, this has never been harder for women to do—they've been raised to be distrustful of men. But that doesn't mean it can't be done. Begin by rejecting the idea that listening to your husband or depending on him in any way means you're weak. By conflating weakness with vulnerability, you create a barrier. *You have to be vulnerable to have love in your life.* Without vulnerability, there can be no trust. And without trust, there can be no intimacy. And without intimacy, well, you get the idea.

So decide today, right now, to face your fears. What are you afraid of that makes you feel the need to take control? What happened in your past that made you skeptical of love? If you're in danger of being hurt, that's one thing. But unfounded fear, or fear that's not a result of anything your husband has done, undermines love. No relationship can last if one person is mentally preparing him or herself to get burned by the other.

ACTION: For one week, practice being a different kind of wife by doing everything opposite of the way you would normally do it. For instance, when your husband says something with which you disagree, say something like, "That's interesting." Where you would normally interject your opinion, don't. Where you would normally complain, say something positive. Where you would normally instruct, ask—preferably with a please or a thank you. Where you would normally say no, say yes. You get the idea. Then see what happens.

2

DECIDE TO STAY

Ceding control is only half the battle. The other half is equally significant: you have to change your attitude toward men and marriage. Your attitude is the *single most important determiner* of your success in life, whether we're talking about your job or your marriage.

Let me restate that because it's so important: Your attitude is *the single most important determiner* of your success in life, whether we're talking about your job or your marriage. Life will throw you a thousand curve balls. So will marriage. But it isn't the curve balls that matter—it's what you do with those curve balls. And what you *do* stems from how you *think*.

Women have robbed Peter to pay Paul. They may be more successful in the professional sphere, but they know next to nothing about love.

So what *are* your views on marriage as an institution? Are they traditional in nature, or do they match the culture's more progressive, cavalier view? The America of today teaches two basic tenets about marriage: that it isn't necessary, and that it needn't be permanent. Marriage and motherhood are also no longer a woman's *raison d'être*. Her career is.

That's a tectonic shift in attitudes in a short period of time. Previous generations of women embraced marriage and all that came with it. They considered love and family life to be the center of life, not a side dish. We hear a lot about how bad things were for women "back in the day." But the truth is, women have robbed Peter to pay Paul.

They may be more successful in the professional sphere, but they know next to nothing about love.

The Happiness Factor

Today's culture teaches that marriage is supposed to make women happy, and that if it doesn't, a wife should leave her marriage and find happiness with someone else. Here's a paragraph from a typical article about marriage, entitled "Confessions of a Semi-Happy Wife":

> Beneath the thumpingly ordinary nature of our marriage— every marriage—runs the silent chyron of divorce.... Thank God for divorce, which may be the last-standing woman's right to choose. One eloquent swing of the ax and happiness is thrust firmly back into our own hands.

It is impossible to overstate the significance of messages like this one. When a woman hits a wall in her marriage, and she will, the culture doesn't give her the tools she needs to climb over it. Instead, this is what she gets: If you're not happy, leave.

Talk about sabotage! Who's never unhappy? And why should becoming a wife (or a husband, for that matter) guarantee one's happiness? Yet this directive—"life's too short; move on if you're unhappy"—is pervasive, and it's tailored specifically to women.

To be clear, I'm not arguing that divorce isn't sometimes necessary. The problem is that we live in a culture that equates divorce with liberation, rather than as a last-ditch solution for extreme circumstances. Ask any honest psychologist, and he or she will tell you divorce is a temporary relief at best. More often than not, divorce creates more problems than it solves.

So let's change the paradigm. Rather than assume divorce is the answer to marital conflict, change your views about marriage itself. For instance, *the purpose of marriage is not to make you happy*. You and you alone are responsible for that.

In the last chapter, we discussed the brain's ability to control behavior. Did you know we're also capable of controlling our thoughts? It's true we can't help what enters our brains—we can't control our feelings, in other words—but we can change the way we think about those feelings. We feel with our hearts, but we think with our brains. So use your brain to overrule your heart.

Make yourself happy.

I have a saying that I keep on prominent display in my office. It reads: "Happiness is something you decide ahead of time." I also keep those Seeds of Happiness lying around. Both help train my brain to be happy. I admit it's not the most romantic route to happiness. It might even sound like I'm forcing myself to be happy. Then again, maybe I'm just being smart.

Harvard scientist Dan Gilbert, author of *Stumbling Upon Happiness*, writes that when it comes to happiness, most people have the "wrong map." Natural happiness, he says, is what happens when people get what they want. That A in school, for instance. Or that car, or that award, or that house. But studies show that getting what we want doesn't actually make us happy—that's why the joy associated with these events is short-lived. It's the reason we need a new happiness fix to help move the feeling along. After about three months, that thing we imagined would make us happy, whatever it was, has virtually no impact on our happiness at all. It was a tease.

Take buying a new car. You know how at first it feels really great? It's so clean and full of new possibilities. But give it a year, and the car starts to lose its vitality. You get used to it. You wake up one day and realize it's just a car, a mode of transportation. It no longer feels the way it did when you bought it. That's because the purchase of the car didn't make you happy. Euphoric, perhaps. But not happy.

So what will you do when the euphoria has waned? You could trade the car in for a new model in order to get the euphoria back. But remember: the joy won't last. That's because the key to happiness lies *in your ability to create it*. Gilbert calls this "synthetic happiness." Synthetic happiness isn't a result of natural origin or happenstance. It's produced.

Too many people think of happiness as something over which they have no control, something that happens *to* them. It's easier that way, for sure—and more fun perhaps. But it doesn't last. And don't you want something that lasts? "In our society, we have a strong belief that synthetic happiness is of an inferior kind. Yet synthetic happiness is every bit as real and enduring as the kind of happiness you stumble upon when you get exactly what you were aiming for."[1]

Ironically, it's women's definition of and expectations for happiness that undermine their own happiness. The best shot any one of us has of being happy—in any domain, but especially in marriage—is to have *no* expectations. Not high, low or medium expectations. None. Rather, go with what you get, or with what you've already chosen, and create a happy life from that. "The psychological immune system works best when we are totally stuck, when we are trapped," writes Gilbert.[2]

That may sound counterintuitive, but it follows the same logic as that put forth by psychologist Barry Schwartz. In *The Paradox of Choice*, he writes, "When a decision is final, we engage in a variety of psychological processes that enhance our feelings about the choice we made relative to the alternatives."[3]

It also reflects something Martha Washington once said: "The greater part of our misery or circumstances depends on our dispositions and not on our circumstances." And finally, what Abraham Lincoln noted: "People are about as happy as they make up their minds to be."

The Green Grass Syndrome, or "Satisficers" vs. "Maximizers"

What keeps alpha females, in particular, from being able to be happy in a less-than-perfect marriage is they insist on having the absolute best at all times. If they don't, they feel they are living a lesser life. This is part and parcel of the alpha female's naturally critical nature. At heart, she's a "maximizer." A maximizer is someone who's rarely satisfied or who cannot make do with less than perfect. You can see how this would be debilitating when it comes to marriage—not just for her but for her husband, who can't possibly measure up to such high standards.

That's why the best thing you can do as a wife is to become a "satisficer." A satisficer concentrates on the reasons she made the decision she did and practices gratitude, or being grateful for the wisdom of that choice. Now if one's choice of husband was wildly stupid—you married a man who's addicted to drugs or alcoholic or who lacks character or basic decency—that's one thing. But assuming that's not the case, focus on why you chose the man you did. Focus on what he brings to the table and be done with it. Don't look for more.

Decide to stay.

You can't switch husbands the way you can switch jobs. If you do, you will leave behind a trail of misery. Each time people remarry, their chances of failure skyrocket. That's not me talking—those are the statistics. *More than 70% of remarriages that involve stepchildren fail.* That bears repeating: more than 70% of remarriages that involve stepchildren fail.

You're simply better off staying with the man you chose in the first place, assuming he's safe and if children are involved. It is infinitely easier to improve an existing marriage than it is to start over from scratch. Because give it enough time, and that marriage will have just as many warts as the first. What will you do then? Become Elizabeth Taylor?

I'm not suggesting divorce is never the answer. It may indeed be. What I'm saying is that divorce is never the answer if the purpose for it is to find happiness with someone else. What I'm saying is that it's possible you're your own worst enemy, that the underlying issue lies within you and not within the marriage.

If that is the case, why not take a new approach, a new attitude, toward to the problems you're having? What if the answer has been there all along and you have yet to take advantage of it? Isn't that worth exploring?

When it comes to marital conflict, which every single married couple on the planet has, the trick is to focus on the problem itself and to not get mired in blame. Blame invariably leads to thoughts about other men, or other relationship scenarios, that you're convinced would be better for you. That is what's known as the Green Grass Syndrome, and it's toxic.

The Green Grass Syndrome, or the propensity to believe a different choice would be better for you than the one you've already made, is debilitating. And it's never been more difficult to avoid. A culture of endless choices and options, as we have today, encourages women to search for something better when they're dissatisfied. It *helps* push women out the door.

I'm not saying women treat marriage lightly or file for divorce the moment there's a crisis. I don't think they do. But without a belief system in place that differs from the one they've absorbed from the culture, they will always land in the same spot. Women are trying to solve problems with the only paradigm they've been offered. (Leave!) And that one doesn't work.

Something our mothers and grandmothers understood that women today do not is this: *You can never get everything you want all wrapped up in one man.* No matter who you end up with, there will always be something missing. Always. "Research has shown that every happy, successful couple has approximately ten areas of 'incompatibility' or disagreement that they will never resolve...If we switch partners, we'll just get ten new areas of disagreement," writes relationship expert Diane Sollee of SmartMarriages.com.[4]

A recent survey of 1,000 married women showed fifty percent of women—50%!—have a "backup husband," or a man who serves as Plan B in case their marriages fail. Talk about undermining your own marriage! These women have created a self-fulfilling prophecy. Fantasizing about a marriage that doesn't exist and preparing for the demise of your actual marriage will almost certainly lead to its death.

It is your attitude that makes the difference. The way we handle conflict when we assume we'll be together "til death do us part" is very different from the way we approach conflict when we assume we can always leave. Technically, no one is stuck—the freedom to divorce will always be there. The trick is to pretend it isn't. "The very option of being allowed to change our minds seems to increase the chances we *will* change our minds. When we can change our minds about decisions, we are less satisfied with them," writes Schwartz.[5]

Constantly asking yourself whether or not you chose well, or whether or not your husband is worthy of you, or whether or not you'd be better off with someone else is disruptive to the marriage. It's like trying to have a conversation with another adult when a toddler is in the room. The constant distraction undermines the goal.

I know it's more challenging to avoid the Green Grass Syndrome today. Hollywood images are forever hailing the Divorced American Female, with either the assumption or the assertion that she was duped by her husband. One rarely sees a Hollywood male on the cover of *People* gloating about his divorce or claiming that his ex made a terrible wife. The message is always the same: wife was wronged by husband and ultimately finds happiness with a better man.

Other people's divorces can have an effect even if they don't come from Hollywood. Research by sociologist James H. Fowler found that if a sibling divorces, we are 22 percent more likely to get divorced ourselves. And when our friends get divorced, it's even more influential: people who had a divorced friend were *147 percent* more likely to get divorced than people whose friends' marriages were intact. It would appear that divorce is contagious.

It takes a great deal of discipline to stay married when divorce is all around you. The only option you have is to reject the Green Grass Syndrome and to become a satisficer. Making comparisons sets up unrealistic expectations, which then set up a false reality. Real life can only be disappointing, as no spouse can possibly measure up. Every flaw he or she has become glaringly obvious.

You ultimately have to accept, or become comfortable with, the fact that you're going to be dissatisfied *to some degree* no matter whom you marry—and that when this happens, someone else's life will always seem more appealing. But it only seems that way from a distance. In reality, that person's life has just as many problems as yours. "This is the difference between marriage and dating: you find a way to be happy with what's happened," says Gilbert.[6]

Find a way to be happy with what's happened.

Decide to stay.

ACTION: By mentally removing the option to get divorced, you allow yourself to stay focused on the marriage and not get bogged down in blame or what-ifs. Making the decision to stay forces your brain to create happiness with the man you've already chosen, rather than imagining a life with someone else. So get rid of the husband of your dreams. Stick with reality, and shoot for contentment. Happiness is fleeting. But contentment is a permanent state.

3

LEARN THE DANCE

It's simple, really: when it comes to love, women hold all the cards. As the relationship-oriented sex, or the relationship "navigator," a woman has the power to steer the ship in the direction she wants it to go. The trick is to steer the ship well.

A good man wants his wife to be happy more than anything else in the world, and he will go to great lengths to make it happen. He'll even support his wife's ideas, plans or opinions if he doesn't agree with them. That's because a husband's number one goal is to please his wife. If he determines his wife cannot be pleased, that's when the marriage is in trouble.

Men are just so much simpler than women. Not simple as in dumb, as is often portrayed in the media. Simple in that they have far fewer needs than we do. What men want most of all is respect, companionship, and sex. If you supply these basics, your husband will do anything for you—slay the dragons, kill the beast, work three jobs, and so on. Men will happily do this if, and only if, they are loved well in return. It is when men are not loved well that problems arise. That is the nature of the male-female dance.

Now I know what you're thinking—that I'm putting everything on you. Not exactly. Your husband is responsible for his own actions. If he chooses to get repeatedly drunk, for instance, it's his job to own up to that behavior and put a stop to it. Same goes for his emotional outbursts, if he has them, or his not coming home when he said he would, or even his having an affair.

What I *am* saying is that men tend to follow women's lead. Your husband's actions are more often than not *re*actions. He's reacting to something you said or did, or to something you didn't say or didn't do. He's reacting to your moods, your gestures, your inflections, and your tone. That's how men are. Your husband wants you to be happy, and when he sees it isn't working he thinks he's failed. That's when he acts out.

To put it another way: a wife is in charge of the puppet strings. If she pulls on the wrong one, she gets a negative response. If she pulls on the right one, she gets a positive response. Once you know this, or more importantly, once you accept it, you realize that if your relationship isn't going well, it is you who needs to change. You need to go first. If you do, the rest will fall into place.

Another way to think about the male-female dance is to consider the game of chess. In chess, the king is the most important piece but also one of the weakest. He can only move one square in any direction—up, down, to the sides, and diagonally. The queen, however, is the most powerful piece. She can move in any one direction—forward, backward, sideways, or diagonally. And how *she* moves affects how he moves.

As a woman, you can respond to this dynamic in one of two ways: you can resent it, or you can embrace it. I used to resent it.

I'd think to myself, *How can I possibly make sure my husband isn't negatively affected by my every mood swing? I'm a Pisces, for God's sake! My moods shift with the wind! Plus, why am I responsible for my husband's reactions?* The whole thing seemed like a whole lot of pressure, not to mention unfair.

> A wife is in charge of the puppet strings. If she pulls on the wrong one, she gets a negative response. If she pulls on the right one, she gets a positive response.

It took me an embarrassingly long time to get it. But once I did, once I accepted that the energy I exude and the way I approach my husband directly affects his response and behavior, I changed my tune. And when I did, something happened. My marriage became a piece of cake. Whatever conflicts we had disappeared overnight. Just like that.

Well, almost like that. It was a lot of stop and go at first. First I'd handle something the "right" way and marvel at the response. Then life would get busy, and I'd resort to my old ways. Sure enough, I'd get a different response. Then I'd make a mental note of how I messed up and make sure to get it right the next time. I still do it.

What makes the transition hard at first isn't the follow-through—it's the remembering to stop and think about it. It takes a lot to change a behavior you've had for life. But once you understand the steps, it becomes a no-brainer. It's like weight loss. Once you realize that sugar and carbs create fat, a light bulb goes off in your head. You've unlocked the code to keeping your weight in check. Even if you fall off the wagon (and you will), you know what to do to get back on track. That's what it's like to love a man. Once you learn how, you're good to go. You have all the tools you need.

But you have to use them.

The first and most important tool is to understand and accept gender differences. If you do not do this, your relationship with your husband will remain mired in conflict. Unfortunately, you've been groomed in a culture of equality—which in modern parlance means sameness. That is the narrative the culture sells.

But you don't have to buy it. Recognizing that men and women are equal but different is the key to lasting love because it removes all frustration—"Why is he doing this?"—as well as the need to blame. There's no reason to get mad anymore because you recognize and appreciate why your husband thinks and behaves as he does.

The verbiage used to represent sex differences, a.k.a. masculinity and femininity, varies. "Alpha and beta" is one set of terms: alpha means masculine, and beta means feminine. But the Chinese use the expression "yin and yang." Yin refers to the feminine, and yang refers to the masculine. The Chinese-English dictionary lists the yin's (or the beta's) qualities as "negative/passive/covert/hidden" and the yang's (or the alpha's) qualities as "positive/active/open/overt." Think of male and female sex organs. Or think of a battery. One part is positive, and the other is negative. In order for the battery to work, both energies must be present.

Masculine energy conquers and cogitates. It likes to do things, and it likes to be alone to think about how to do those things. Feminine energy nurtures and verbalizes. It likes to talk, and to be pampered and doted upon. That's why feminine energy is the receiver of masculine energy. It's why men typically make the first move in a relationship and why the man asks the woman for her hand in marriage, rather than the other way around. The male acts, and the female responds.

The fact that men are *capable* of nurturing and women are *capable* of conquering doesn't change the fact that this is typically not where each sex's natural energy flows. Despite what the culture tells you, gender is not a social construct. Or at least, it's not primarily or only a social construct. Men and women are as different as night and day, and these differences are a deeply rooted part of evolutionary biology.

I was reminded of this when I passed my neighbor recently who was walking with her two young children, a boy and a girl. The baby girl was in a stroller, and her three-year-old brother was walking next to the stroller wearing a Superman costume. There was no party. It wasn't Halloween. The boy just wanted to be Superman. He wanted to be a hero.

When this boy's sister is his age, she will be much more likely to put on a princess costume, expressing her desire to be loved and cared for, than she will be to put on a Superwoman costume and pretend to conquer the world. She might put on a Superwoman costume, and that's fine. She might even wear both a princess costume and a Superwoman costume. But she is still *far more likely* to choose the princess costume. That is the reality of human nature.

It's true there's variation within the masculine/feminine framework. Not every man is the same degree of alpha and not every woman is the same degree of beta. But one thing is certain: for a relationship to last, both partners cannot bring the same energy to the table. "One of the basic agreements a couple makes is who's the male and who's the female. It usually breaks down along obvious gender lines, but not always … either you're providing the female energy and Mr. Charming is providing the male, or you're assuming the male role and he, the female," writes basketball star-turned author Gabby Reece in *My Foot Is Too Big for the Glass Slipper.*[1]

Male Nature, aka the Alpha

With so much focus on the American female, male nature is often cast aside or at the very least misunderstood. But to have a successful marriage, a woman must understand how men think and behave. One of the things parents learn early on is that introducing gender-neutral toys—which has become a fad these days—does not make a child more like the opposite sex.

In *Taking Sex Differences Seriously*, Dr. Steven E. Rhoads tells of the story of a mother who wrote about her "Herculean effort to bring up a peaceable male three-year-old in left-leaning Berkeley. At home, the only television her son watched was *Sesame Street*. There were no toy guns in his home or in the homes of his closest friends. The local toy store didn't even carry toy guns. Nevertheless, the boy seemed to be obsessed with guns. He quickly learned that tinker toys make wonderful guns, and one of his male friends found that even waffles could be used to shoot his dad at breakfast."[2]

Any one of my friends or family members who has a son can attest to this. It is common knowledge among mom circles as well. Masculinity is very, very real—and despite what the culture teaches, it is not a bad thing. Masculinity isn't just about a man's (or a boy's) desire to fight. The most significant aspect of masculine nature is a man's need to be useful, or to feel a sense of purpose. As clinical psychologist Shawn T. Smith writes in his most recent book, *The Practical Guide to Men*, "If there's one single measure of a man card, it's the expectation that the man produces more than he consumes." His reward, he adds, is "praise, respect and admiration."[3]

Feminine nature feels, dreams, and empathizes, whereas masculine nature *acts* (and *reacts*). It builds things and makes things, like forts or money or skyscrapers. It figures things out and comes up with answers. Men have a visceral need to know what they're doing and to be right. Being a leader is part of who they are and how they're made. So, let them lead.

This is where modern women struggle. They've been taught to do everything themselves and to be leaders to boot. But being a leader in the marketplace is different from being the leader in your marriage. Even being the leader of your children, as an at-home mom, is different from being the leader in your marriage.

Women in previous generations understood men. Take my "Aunt" Joan, who's not technically my aunt—she's the wife of my first cousin once removed, whose name is Ned. Ned and Joan have been married 57 years, and one of the things I love to hear Joan talk about are the ways she has learned to deal with Ned, or with men in general, over the years. One story she told me had to do with Ned's driving. Ned isn't exactly the best driver in the world—he tends to drive about a foot behind the car in front of him. For years Joan put up with this behavior and would often ask Ned not to drive so close to other cars. But nothing she said worked.

So Joan got creative. She began to tell Ned, every time they were headed somewhere together, that she was going to drive herself and just meet him there. She didn't say it in a nasty or an angry way. She just made up some excuse as to why she needed to drive separately. (She had to run an errand or drop something off on the way, and so on.)

Joan did this for a period of two weeks until Ned caught on to what she was doing. Finally, he went to her and said, "If I promise not to drive too close to the car in front of me, will you drive with me?" Joan said she'd be willing to think about that, but of course she relented. Sometimes you have to use a little psychology to get what you want, and women are much better at this than men are.

Joan then told me a similar story about one of her friends—let's call her Sally. Sally is married to a high alpha whose job puts him in a strong leadership position. Problem is, he had a tendency to talk down to Sally or to even be verbally abusive. Every time the two of them had a conversation, he wouldn't let Sally get a word in edgewise. After years of trying to get him to be more respectful or to be a better communicator, Sally decided she'd had enough. So she wrote her husband a letter and explained to him that letter-writing would be the way they'd communicate from now on.

For several weeks Sally and her husband had no verbal communication. She would go into another room or leave the house if he tried to talk to her. She would only talk to him via letters, and her husband was forced to do the same because that's the only way she'd listen to what he had to say. Well, by the third week he'd had enough—said he couldn't keep up with this. So he was forced to change his ways.

It is impossible to imagine a modern woman taking this same approach with her husband. She is far more likely to file for divorce and to cite emotional abuse. And while she may feel justified, where does it get her? If she's married with kids, it just makes her life worse. In the end, Sally got what she wanted without having to go through all that. Seems to me she's the winner.

> You can't change human nature. The more you fight it, the more miserable you'll be.

Another great example is the matriarch in the film *My Big Fat Greek Wedding*. When Maria Portokalos's daughter Toula gets excited about an opportunity to work at her aunt's travel agency, she decides to broach the subject with her father—an old-school Greek who's obsessed with the idea of Toula marrying a Greek man and making lots of Greek babies. But Maria, Toula's mother, knows the only way to get her husband to agree to Toula working at the agency (yes, I know it's ridiculous they need the father's approval, but stay with me) is if he thinks the idea is his.

So one day Maria, Toula, and the aunt are sitting in the family's restaurant with the dad, complaining about the aunt needing help at her agency and not knowing anyone who can do the job. The father says, "I know! Hire Nicky!" (Nick is his son, Toula's brother.) But Maria says Nick doesn't know how to use a computer. Then the three women pretend they have no idea what to do. Even the dad is stumped for a moment until he remembers that Toula has been taking computer classes. So he says, "Aha! Toula can do it!" And Maria fawns all over her husband for coming up with such a great idea, as though she hadn't thought of it herself.

There are loads of similar exchanges in that film that teach great lessons about men and marriage. But you need to have a sense of humor to appreciate them. Many women today, particularly young women, would take offense at the idea that a wife should have to "cater" to male nature by appealing to her husband's need to be in charge. I understand that, and I probably felt this way at one point myself.

But time has a way of changing things, at least for those who want their marriages to last. There are things about human nature we cannot change, and the more you fight against them the more miserable you'll be. There's a reason my Aunt Joan, along with Sally and the matriarch in *My Big Fat Greek Wedding* have been married for decades.

Another aspect of male nature is that a man must be "read." You have to study your husband carefully because he isn't going to give you much to work with. Mothers of boys know this all too well. My son will not voluntarily verbalize how his day went, nor will he share what he thinks or how he feels about something on command. He will, however, tell you when he's good and ready. But it has to be on his terms. It's the same way with your husband.

But don't confuse a man's silence or simplicity with a lack of depth. Don't assume that because your husband doesn't express emotions the way you do that he lacks the ability to feel things deeply. Men *are* deep. They just don't talk about their feelings every time they have them. They also have fewer feelings than women do. And when they arise, a man will generally stew about them first. But if his feelings are of a negative nature, and they aren't given an outlet—if you rarely listen to your husband when he's ready to talk—over time he may engage in stupid behavior. You can get mad about this, or you can accept it and behave accordingly.

Hands down, the most important thing to understand about men is their need for respect. Respect is the glue that makes the dance work. Everything else, and I mean *everything* else, flows from there. In the same way you crave your husband's love and attention, he craves your respect. If he has it, the relationship runs like a well-oiled machine. If he doesn't, the relationship falls apart. At work, your husband gets respect without having to ask for it.

He's counted on to get a job done and isn't (necessarily) told how to do it. You need to produce this same environment at home, as it will, in turn, precipitate the type of behavior you desire from him.

Sadly, we live in an era in which male disrespect is palpable. In the span of a few short decades, America has managed to demote its men from respected providers and protectors of the family to superfluous buffoons. "Name a sitcom from 1970 forward that depicts a strong, responsible, intelligent father figure. Fathers in sitcoms are good-hearted, but they are also depicted as immature, dumb, lazy and incompetent. Do we seriously believe this drumbeat of messages has no impact?" writes *New York Times* reader Allan Bird.

It has major impact. Today's sitcoms, *and* commercials, routinely paint a portrait of the idiot husband whose wife is smarter and more capable than he. Ward Cleaver is long gone, and in his place is The New Dad: unemployed, unaware, and thoroughly emasculated. To think this does not have an effect on everyone is to bury one's head in the sand. Cultural messages either support or undermine the way people live. They are very, very important.

It is no coincidence that as the culture moved away from respect for men as providers, defenders, and supporters of women, wives began to lose respect for their husbands. This is a major problem since husbands, as a rule, are inherently respectful of their wives. Husbands don't typically tell their wives what to do, no doubt because they don't like to be told what to do themselves.

A husband views being told what to do by his wife as disrespect. He thinks it means you don't believe he's capable of whatever it is you've told him to do—which, let's face it, you don't. That's why you're telling him how to do it. What happens then is your relationship becomes imbalanced: he's *not* telling you what to do as a sign of respect, but you're not reciprocating. Over time, this wears the marriage down until there's nothing left.

Of course, wives who tell their husbands what to do don't view their behavior as a sign of disrespect. They see it as "helping" their husbands be all they can be! Plus, a husband's behavior is a reflection of his wife, so she has a vested interest in what other people see when they look at her husband. Because of this, many wives consider it their *job* to lead their husbands in the same way they lead their children or in the same way they lead people at work.

But men don't want to be led.

Another way a wife can be disrespectful is by dismissing the work her husband does. No matter how much gender roles have changed, men still have a visceral need to provide for their families—that their wives may be employed doesn't change this fact. Most men don't view their wives' income as indispensable—unless the roles are completely reversed, which is rare.

A great book by Dr. Emerson Eggerichs titled *Love and Respect* gets to the heart of this issue. He writes that many married couples get on what he calls the "crazy cycle." What women want most of all, he says, is love. And what men want is respect. When both are present in the relationship, the marriage works. When they're denied, it doesn't. "Ironically, the deepest need of the wife—to feel loved—is undermined by her disrespect."[4]

Since your husband wants to make you happy, he will do whatever it is you want; but he doesn't want to be told when or how to do it. He doesn't want to feel as though you demanded it of him. He wants to feel as though he chose to be of service to you, that he improved your life or made it immeasurably better or easier.

Let's say you want him to paint the bathroom. The best thing to do is to point out how much you would love and appreciate the new color. Don't nag your husband to do it. Don't demand that he do it. Don't even notice when he doesn't do it after he said he would, which used to be a big problem in our house. Just strategically place that jar of paint somewhere where he'll see it. Then say something complimentary or do something nice for him. Don't go on and on with your request—he heard you the first time. Just say it and move on.

Here's another example. Let's say you're tired of the fact that your husband doesn't keep his side of the bedroom clean. Don't say, "You never keep your side of the bedroom clean, and I'm sick of it!" Say something like, "I feel so much better when the bedroom is clutter free. I can think clearly, and that makes me so much happier."

In other words, instead of starting a conversation with, "You never," start it with, "I miss" or "I'd like …" The goal is to make the request or comment about *you* instead of about him, to focus on what you want or like and not on the ways in which your husband is inadequate.

For instance, I found I really liked it when my husband was the one to fill the Keurig coffee machine with water so it's full when I wake up in the morning. Then I thought to myself how much I would like it if he did that every day. But instead of asking him if he would do it on a regular basis, or worse, telling him to do it on a regular basis, I just said, "I really love it when you fill the Keurig machine with water. It's one less thing for me to have to do in the morning." Men will respond to this approach because they love to lighten our load.

See, once you connect the dots, once you understand the male-female dance, marriage becomes a piece of cake. Once you accept that your husband's response depends on your approach, you're empowered—because you know what to do. And when you get what you want as a result, and when he gets what he wants as a result, sticking with it is even easier. You'll continue to mess up, of course. But you just get right back on the saddle.

Naturally, all of this assumes you do respect your husband. If you don't, or if you're not sure if you do, here's a good gauge: *Do you believe you married down?* Because if you feel superior to your husband, you probably don't respect him. If that is not how you feel, if you do respect your husband but you still order him around, he will not see the difference.

If you do think you're superior to your husband, go to the closest mirror you can find, look in it, and accept that you're not all that. You are not better or smarter or wiser than your husband. Your way isn't the *right* way—it's just *one* way. You aren't the only person in the relationship who can dress well, or grocery shop, or pay the bills, or be a parent. If you think your husband isn't capable of those things, it may be because you're always one step ahead of him. Or it may be you expect him to be just like you.

Your husband can never be you.

A woman must understand male nature if she wants to find peace with a man. Unfortunately, the younger you are the more difficult this will be because we live in a culture that denigrates men. This has in turn caused many women to act haughty, as though they're better than men. Women today don't want to use psychology to accommodate the male psyche—they'd rather believe they're superior and then blame men for everything that goes wrong.

Since that gets you nowhere, you will at some point be faced with making one of two choices.

You can file for divorce.

Or you can learn the dance.

ACTION: There are two ways to approach wifedom. You can say to yourself, "It's not fair that I have to steer the ship!" Or you can say to yourself, "Wow, so I hold all the power?" The great thing about the latter is that you don't have to wait around for your husband to change. You have the ability to create the kind of marriage you want all by yourself. So just do it. Grab the power.

4

OWN YOUR FEMININE
(OR YOUR INNER BETA)

In order for your husband to own his masculinity, you'll have to own your femininity. If you're too masculine, one of two things will happen. Your husband will rise to meet your energy level, which will result in conflict; or he will step back and let you take over. There's literally nowhere else for him to go.

You may think your husband isn't very manly. But unless your relationship started out with your calling him and inviting him out on a date, or your asking him to marry you, that isn't likely. It's far more likely that somewhere along the line you smothered his masculinity.

Remember: men don't like to fight with women. So a man who's married to an alpha female is stuck between wanting to please his wife and feeling the need to be in charge. And while you may like to be in control *in general*, you don't really want to be in control of your man, right? What you want is for your husband to *be* a man.

To do that, you have to be a woman.

So how, exactly, does an alpha female become more feminine, or more beta? By making up your mind to do so, and then doing it. (That's something alphas do well!) Your inner beta does exist—it's just dormant because you haven't allowed it to express itself. I don't believe you were aggressive and bossy when you and your husband first met, or even when the two of you were dating or just married. Your strong personality came through, I'm sure; but I bet you smiled a lot and doted on your husband. I bet he fell in love with a perfectly nice woman. Men don't typically marry bitches.

On the contrary, men gravitate toward women who are nice and who are easy to please. A man will date a domineering woman—he'll certainly have sex with her!—but he won't envision a future with her. He won't see her as the mother of his children.

Now when I say men like women who are nice and easy to please, I don't mean men are looking for a pushover or are looking for a woman who has no opinions or life of her own. This is a common misperception of beta females. Being feminine does not mean you lack an identity or that you're an appendage of your husband. That's the narrative the culture sells, but it doesn't mean it's true.

Indeed, you've been taught from birth to be wary of men and to exercise your "bitch" muscle in order to prove your value to men and to society. As a result, women associate strength with being bossy or even bitchy. Media personality Terri Trespicio is a great example of this modern conundrum. In 2012 Trespicio graced the cover of *Boston* magazine to extol the merits of singlehood. But two years later in a YouTube video, she concedes she's missing out by not settling down and, in a bold and courageous admission, says she's the one with the problem.

"I'm the first to admit I'm not easy. And part of the problem is that I have gone in trying to win…I've always thought that by being super independent and by proving to potential mates that I didn't need anyone that I would be very attractive—because you always hear that men don't like needy, clingy women. And so it's always been my goal to not be needy."[1]

Trespicio is correct that men don't like clingy women (though I would argue this goes both ways), but being clingy and being vulnerable are not the same. Vulnerability is a turn-on; clinginess is not. Just as being smart is a turn-on, but being a know-it-all is not. And just as being self-reliant is important, but not if your man feels superfluous as a result.

If I had to guess, I'd say the point at which your marriage became less complementary and more competitive was when motherhood took over. At that point, you probably stopped being your husband's partner and became his mother instead. That's typically how it happens.

Fortunately, men's devotion to their wives tends to be as strong as their devotion to their mothers—which means wives are given plenty of leeway. Most men don't leave their marriages, or even talk about leaving, unless life has become unbearable or he has fallen in love with someone else. (If your husband *has* mentioned divorce, that's a definite cue it's time to shape up—assuming it's not too late. Ideally, you won't get to this point.) A husband will, however, tune out or turn away if his wife has become too much like a man.

The way to avoid this is to own your feminine.

In layman's terms, this means you need to be nicer. You also need to smile a lot—daily would be good—and get excited about having sex. You don't have to cook and clean, but it'd be nice if you didn't feel threatened or put upon every time you wind up in the kitchen. Or in the laundry room. Your husband will even do those chores himself, as long as you don't tell him how to do them or demand that it be on your timetable. That's when the problems start.

Being a shrew, aka a nag or a bitch, is a surefire path to marital hell. Fortunately, I don't think my behavior as a wife reached bitch status. Still, I wasn't feminine. And I needed to be.

If you Google the word *feminine*, this is the first definition that pops up: "having qualities or an appearance traditionally associated with women, especially delicacy and prettiness." Dig a little further, and you'll find this at Dictionary.com: "having qualities traditionally ascribed to women, such as sensitivity or gentleness."

Delicate. Sensitive. Gentle. None of those words describes me. I'm clumsy, for one thing. I trip over things because I move so quickly in an effort to be expedient. (I get things done! I make things happen!) My daughter says I drive a car as though I were being chased by cops. And when my mother was alive, she was always harping on me to slow down. When I was young she used to say it was like I had a "genie" inside me that had to get out. At one point teachers suggested I be on Ritalin. So clearly, my hyperactive ways are nothing new.

But never in a million years would it have occurred to me that the way I moved could negatively affect my marriage. But it did! There's nothing feminine about running around like a chicken with your head cut off. Perhaps it's no big deal if you're single (although if we're being honest, it isn't healthy); but if you're married, it is a big deal. Why?

Because men like calmness. That is, in part at least, what femininity represents. Your husband wants to come home at the end of the day to a peaceful environment. To him, home represents a place of refuge. To you, home is a bit different. It's a refuge, too, but it's more than that.

As a female, you're more invested in the home—even if you work outside of it. It's a reflection of who you are. And when you're there, you take ownership of your home in the way only a female can. It's your domain. Keeping up with it is important to you, which is why you typically don't rest when you're there.

When it comes to the home, most men don't expect things to be "just so," nor do they hone in on the details of home management. This marital dynamic is one of the reasons we hear so much from women about who's doing what when it comes to household chores and child care. Women are running around on speed these days, and men can't keep up. Nor do they want to.

A stressful environment just isn't conducive to love, no matter who's doing the running around. But let's face it: it's almost always the wife. Even a mental image of a husband and father running around at home is funny. You just don't see that.

> Being feminine isn't just about how a woman dresses or even how she spends her days. Being feminine is a state of mind. It's an attitude.

Ironically, I never thought of myself as *un*feminine—which, in hindsight, seems crazy. Of course I wasn't feminine! But I honestly didn't see it. After all, I used to be a teacher, which is a female-dominated profession; I've been home with my children since they were born; I have zero interest in sports (with the exception of watching my son play hockey); and I do very little yard work. Those are all stereotypical female traits.

But I *am* ambitious, there's no question about that. Plus I don't like to shop or to gossip. I don't even have nice nails! And if someone comes to me with a problem, I can't just sit there and listen—I want to solve the problem. I must help solve! That's the alpha in me.

What I eventually learned was that being feminine isn't just about how a woman dresses or even how she spends her days. Being feminine is a state of mind. It's an attitude. And anyone can develop an attitude, no matter what his or her tendencies may be.

So what is a beta wife like? Well, for one thing, she's easy to please, which makes her easy to love. She also trusts her husband's judgment rather than tells him what to do. She knows when, and when not, to speak up. And she relies on her softer, more vulnerable side—as well as her intuitive emotional skills—when communicating with her husband. (Think Joan, Sally, or Maria Portokalos.)

To get a visual comparison of the alpha and the beta female, consider Kate Gosselin from the reality show *Kate Plus 8* (formerly known as *Jon & Kate Plus Eight*). Gosselin is the quintessential alpha female. Of course she's not a wife anymore, which is no coincidence. (In fact, before she and her husband got divorced, my husband said, "That marriage will never last.") Gosselin's tone, words, and body language toward her ex-husband Jon were shockingly disrespectful and condescending. I said earlier there are various degrees of alphas. On a scale from 1 to 10, Kate Gosselin is a 15.

Another example, if you've seen *The Proposal*, is the character Margaret (played by Sandra Bullock). Margaret is a major alpha female. So is the wife in *Spanglish* (played by Téa Leoni) and Mary in *Downton Abbey*. As in *Leap Year*, each of these characters represents how the typical alpha female refuses to yield to a man. In each case, the male lead is forced to take the alpha female down a notch or two. He has to help her find her soft underbelly so she can stop being such a bitch. In *Downton Abbey*, that role fell to Tom.

Now with any one of these alpha female images in mind, consider Audrey Hepburn. Audrey Hepburn was the epitome of femininity. The way she dressed, the way she walked, the way she spoke, just the way she carried herself in general was exceedingly feminine.

But here's the thing: you don't have to dress, or even talk or walk, like Audrey Hepburn to harness your inner beta. Nor do you need to become June Cleaver. Becoming more feminine doesn't *necessarily* mean you have to dress differently, or that you even walk or talk more slowly—although those things don't hurt. It certainly doesn't mean you never hold a job or you never speak your mind. It just means you stop directing everyone's traffic.

That's not to say attire doesn't matter. In fact, the more feminine you look, the more attractive you will be to your husband. For instance, men love high heels. In fact, high heels are the perfect representation of feminine power. I don't wear heels often enough at all, which is probably why when I do put them on, I'm immediately aware of a shift. I'm sure you know what I'm talking about. If not, throw a pair of those babies on and go out on a few errands. If you pay attention, you'll see the number of men whose eyes either gravitate in your direction or who stay fixed on you. Men are made to respond to feminine images. Literally: the visual and spatial region of the right cerebral cortex is thicker in males than it is in females. Men cannot *not* look at you.

That's power.

And it applies to feminine behavior as well. Feminine behavior is soft on the outside and strong on the inside. Being soft on the outside is not the same thing as being a mouse. Men love women who are fun and feisty and who know their own mind! But they don't want a fire-eating dragon. And they don't want a woman's strength to overpower theirs, not because they can't handle it (as you'll hear many women say) but because they don't want to handle it. They don't want to fight with you. Besides, you don't need to prove anything to your husband—he already knows how valuable you are. That's why he married you.

As a man named Chuck wrote on my website: "A strong woman is awesome. But she must be inviting and be able to mesh into an actual relationship. Needing to dominate and overpower, that is a no go." And from Jim: "Successful women are not intimidating to me. The problem is that many women are becoming too manly. I'd rather have an independent woman who is not clingy, but I usually find women who think I need a boss, thus negating my own independence." And from Jonathan: "Be careful of trading any femininity to compete in the world. Surely needed, yes. But you're paying a price for it."

Surrendering to your femininity does not make you weak.

It makes you smart.

For a long time, I embraced my alpha personality as though it were a baby in need of protection. Why should I have to change? Who would I be if I changed? And how could I be someone different, even if I wanted to? But over a period of time, I got tired of my alpha nature bumping up against my husband's. We were like two bulls hanging out in the same pen together, and it wasn't peaceful.

I was exhausted. Desperate. And I realized something, or more likely some*one*, had to give. One of us had to take on the more feminine role, and I had no desire for that person to be my husband. He's already a perfect mix of alpha and beta.

To be honest, I've always believed I hit the jackpot when I met Bill. My cousin Anne once told me, after she and her husband had spent an evening at our home years ago, that her husband told her on the drive home that night that Bill has "mastered the art of jiujitsu." Jiujitsu is a Japanese martial art representing one's ability to manipulate the opponent's force against himself rather than confronting it with one's own force.

I cannot think of a better description of my husband. Bill accepts my strong-willed nature and has no desire to compete with it. But if I step over the line, he's the first one to tell me. He just isn't easily intimidated. I often call Bill a chameleon because you can literally take that man anywhere, to the queen's table or to a soup kitchen, and he'll fit right in. I love that about him.

Bill's convinced our relationship works because he's a beta on the outside and an alpha on the inside, whereas I'm an alpha on the outside and a beta on the inside. That's probably true. I'm much more bark than bite, and he's much more passionate and competitive than he can sometimes appear.

Here are his results from the alpha-beta personality quiz:

You are a good mixture of Alpha and Beta; you probably get along with everyone and are well liked. You are confident without being overbearing. As a cooperative person, you may prefer letting your partner take the lead—but you are not a pushover. You will partner well with a strong Alpha since you can hold your own. However, you will be comfortable in a stable, secure relationship with another person like yourself.

Bill is like a giant teddy bear with boxing gloves in his pockets. If you need a visual and you've seen *Downton Abbey* (okay, so now you know I love *Downton Abbey*), think Mr. Bates. My husband is Mr. Bates. Definitely balder, but still. Bill is big and strong and proud. He's also a sports fanatic. Oh, and did I mention he hates to be told what to do? Ah yes, I think I did.

A man or a woman can be strong and still be nice.

But he's definitely a beta at heart. He loves art and poetry, for one thing, and he's very attuned to other people's thoughts and behavior. In another life, he'd make an excellent psychologist. He's also a genuinely nice guy, and nice guys can sometimes get a bad rap. The assumption is that the nicer the guy is, the weaker he is. But just as niceness doesn't mean weakness in a female, it doesn't mean weakness in a male. A man or a woman can be strong and still be nice.

In fact, betas radiate an inner strength that belies their persona. The Urban Dictionary writes this about beta males: "Beta males don't buy into stereotypes about male behavior … they have zero interest in keeping up with the Joneses and tend to choose careers that allow them to be more involved at home." What makes (the right kind of) beta male so well-suited to the alpha female is that he isn't blinded by ambition and can thus strike a balance between his professional and his personal life. He is, at heart, a family man.

"Beta males make great husbands," notes the Urban dictionary. "They do more in the house, and probably in the bedroom, since they know how to hasten the greater good…The beta has poetry in him, and a touch of youthful idealism. He's sure of who he is and isn't constantly trying to prove his value in materialistic terms… The beta can earn a lot of money, or a little, but the money's not the thing. He profits because he works well with others."

This is all true about my husband, but he's still very masculine. And testosterone makes men aggressive and driven to win. The male hormone vasopressin is also important. It promotes territoriality and is the reason men don't like to lose an argument. It is therefore easier for women to temper their alpha-like ways than it is for men to temper theirs. Women in general have far less testosterone.

If you get nothing else out of this book, I hope you get this: *do not hold on to your personality as though it's your life's work.* Just because you're inclined toward a certain behavior, just because it's your natural way, doesn't mean you have to embrace it as though it were gold. Our culture spends a lot of time teaching people, especially women, to love and accept themselves as they are, as though they never need to change a thing. But that's ridiculous! What's the point of living year to year in the exact same state, as though you never need to improve anything? It's arrogant to suggest people are fabulous just the way they are. If something about your personality or behavior isn't helpful to your life or to your relationship, get rid of it. You're not giving up who you are. You're just being smart.

Besides, it's liberating to become more beta. Yes: liberating. Self-reliance is exhausting. Making all the decisions is exhausting.

Driving the car, literally or figuratively, is exhausting. Once you stop, once you let go of your need to rule the roost or to have the last word, something bigger happens.

Life becomes infinitely lighter.

There's peace where there used to be war.

ACTION: For the next few days, be soft instead of hard. Be nice instead of a nag. Let your husband do things for you that you're capable of doing but would rather not do. Smile a lot. Compliment him, and thank him for whatever he does on the home front, even if it's something you expect him to do. Basically, pretend it's opposite day and do the reverse of whatever it is you're tempted to do. And then see what happens.

WHO'S THE IDEAL MATE FOR THE ALPHA FEMALE?

In the book *What Women Want—What Men Want*, author and anthropologist John Townsend writes that alpha females (though he doesn't use this term) "continue to show precisely the same preferences in sexuality and mate selection that we see in more traditional women." In other words, alpha females want the same thing beta females do: an alpha male!

But two alphas won't work. And most alpha males prefer betas, which means beta females get first dibs on alpha males. So what option is left for the alpha female who wants to be married?

She either changes her preference in a mate, or she changes herself.

If she's smart, she'll do both.

The ideal mate for an alpha female is a beta male who's strong in his own right but who doesn't need to assert himself in the way an alpha does. A beta male's strength lies in his class and in his dignity. He's fine being married to a strong-willed woman—in fact, he likes it—but he would never let her run all over him. He laughs and enjoys her feistiness, but he commands her respect. Moreover, he likes being her tamer. And she likes it, too.

The film *Far from the Madding Crowd*, set in Victorian England, is an excellent example of this dynamic. When Gabriel, the male protagonist, meets Bathsheba, the female protagonist, he is smitten and asks her to marry him. (Getting married in those days was apparently a much quicker process.) But Bathsheba says she's too strong and independent to marry. Then, as a way of testing Gabriel, to whom she is very much attracted, she says, "If I were ever to marry, I'd want somebody to tame me, and you'd never be able to do it. You'd grow to despise me."

To which Gabriel says, "I would not. Ever."

Then, for the remainder of the film Gabriel is juxtaposed with two other men as possibilities for Bathsheba's future. One is Mr. Boldwood, who's the richest man in the area but who's also 100% beta. (An odd combination, to be sure.) He effectively begs Bathsheba to marry him, going so far as to tell her he doesn't mind if she marries him out of pity.

The other man is Sergeant Troy, a reckless but sexy soldier who loves danger and drink. He's the party boy alpha, and Bathsheba is convinced she's found her match since Troy is equal to her in spirit and temperament. But Bathsheba learns the hard way that Troy has no substance. He throws his weight around, for one thing, and he lacks character.

In the end, Bathsheba comes to her senses just as Gabriel is headed to America for good. It is only then she realizes it is Gabriel she loves; and so this time, it is she who goes after him. In the final scene, she manages to convince Gabriel that she loves him, and they walk off into the sunset. But the telling part of the exchange is that Bathsheba is forced to let down her guard and surrender her will to Gabriel.

The reason I say an alpha female will ideally do both—change her preference in a mate *and* change herself—is because if she just chooses a beta and doesn't let her guard down, she will emasculate her partner. And when that happens, both are miserable. He loses his manhood, and she no longer wants him. It's a lose lose.

5

SERVE FOR THE SAKE OF SERVING

In the film *Away From Her*, a couple (played by Julie Christie and Gordon Pinsent) who've been married for decades face the wife's eventual slide into Alzheimer's. It's a heart-wrenching film, but the takeaway is profound: "falling in love" and real love are two very different things.

At one point in the film, early on before the Alzheimer's sets in, Fiona, the wife, says to her husband Grant, "I think people are too demanding. People want to be in love every single day. What a liability." And at another point, Grant is talking to an aide at the memory care facility where Fiona resides and says to the aide, "It's curious, all that madly in love business. I hear myself tell the story and it sounds so crucial. But compared to what we ended up with, all that seems so superficial somehow."[1]

To be "madly in love," or to be "in love," is an enormously popular idea. But it has nothing to do with love. To be "in love" the way we all are at the beginning of a relationship is just an infatuation period. That in itself never lasts, as much as we'd like it to because it's fun and it feels good. But what it can lead to—real love—is even better. It just takes years to get there.

In the film, there's a lot of flashback to the early days of the couple's marriage—including a time when Grant, a retired professor, had an affair with one of his students. Fiona doesn't leave him, and part of her "reward" for sticking it out is an intensely devoted husband. Their marriage weathered the storm, and Grant was faithful from that point on.

Fast forward several decades. Fiona's dementia sets in, and she checks into a facility. After some time passes, she becomes attached to another dementia patient—a man she tells Grant she knew decades earlier, though it isn't clear whether or not this is true—and Grant is forced to watch as the relationship unfolds. Though it practically killed him to watch his wife's growing attachment to another man, Grant ultimately embraced the relationship for Fiona's sake.

That's love.

To love is to serve. It's something you give, not something you get. To that end, I'm going to suggest you do something that isn't very chic. I'm going to suggest you serve your husband.

Retro, I know. But the truth is, marriage is nothing more than a big, fat, giant exercise in learning to get over yourself. This is true for both sexes. There's only one thing. Men are programmed to serve the woman they love—they love to take care of their wife's needs. Women, on the other hand, have been specifically groomed to never serve a man.

Or at least, alpha females don't. The alpha female tends to live according to *her* needs and plans, not her husband's. To the degree that she's able to do so depends on where she falls on the spectrum. An alpha wife who's a 10 or higher—i.e. the Kate Gosselins of the world—have a lot of work to do if they want to learn how to love. But a lesser alpha female won't struggle as much. For instance, I have a friend who's definitely an alpha female, yet doing for others comes naturally to her. Her alpha-ness has more to do with her high achieving, perfectionist style than anything else. She's intimidating, but she's neither bitchy nor entitled. I'd say she's maybe a 6 or a 7.

> To love is to serve. It means putting the needs of the other person ahead of your own.

Though I've never polled all the alpha females in the world, I choose to believe most are like my friend and not like Kate Gosselin. That is the assumption I've made in writing this book. Women in previous generations had an easier time serving, or loving, their husbands because America wasn't the wealthy nation it is today—and wealth has a tendency to make us more selfish. You've probably heard the adage that the people who have the least give the most. It's like that. Our mothers and grandmothers didn't know a world that catered to their every comfort and convenience. When you live through wars or a Depression, sacrifice is inevitable. A life of sacrifice is simply more conducive to love.

That's one of the reasons women in those days had an easier time being married than those who've never had to struggle. When you're used to having the best, nothing is ever good enough—you always want more. This is what it means to be entitled, and it can wreak havoc on a marriage. Your chances of success are much greater if you're comfortable making do with less, or even doing without. Because ultimately, that is what marriage will ask of you.

Sometimes you will have to love, or serve, your husband even if he doesn't deserve it, or even when you don't feel like it. Truly loving someone means you serve him regardless of what his behavior is like. (This does not apply if your husband is abusive, mentally ill, or addicted to drugs or alcohol—but then this book isn't for you anyway.) You just stay focused on yourself and what you're doing without worrying about him. You don't tally up a score; you choose to love, regardless of what your husband chooses. The beauty of this plan is that most husbands rise to the standards their wives have set. Again, that is the male-female dance.

Author and scholar Jennifer Roback Morse, Ph.D., learned this the hard way. In a speech she gave some years ago, Morse explained to her audience that she once fell victim to the feminist tenet that says a married woman is a mere appendage of her husband. "I took the unexceptional statement that wives are not doormats to mean I have the right, possibly the duty, to stand up for myself inside the marriage. I had come to believe that my dignity as a modern woman depended upon prevailing in disagreements that would arise between my husband and myself."

Perhaps you harbor this same notion, whether you absorbed it from the culture or from your upbringing. It doesn't matter where you got it. The point is, do you feel compelled to stand your ground at all times in the marriage? Is your knee-jerk reaction to the suggestion that you should serve your husband, or do something he suggests with which you may not agree, to become defensive?

If so, turn the scenario around. Do *you* expect your husband to serve *you*? Do you expect him to do something you suggest with which he doesn't agree? I bet it happens all the time. That's because a man's desire to serve his wife is instinctive. His need to make you happy is so automatic he'll let you "win" just to keep the peace. And he'll do it over and over again—until he breaks. Then you have a problem.

What Morse learned the hard way is that the feminist worldview is antithetical to love because its focus is solely on women: their needs, their wants, their desires, and their rights. Love can't possibly be sustained with an attitude like that. Here is a small portion of Morse's speech:

> What did I think love was anyhow? I knew I wanted my husband to accept me as I am, to give me emotional support and encouragement. I wanted him to accept any criticism from me about his faults and failings. At the same time, I demanded he be completely tolerant of any shortcomings of mine. (In my parlance, he had character flaws; I just had shortcomings.)
>
> I was measuring the relationship by what he did for *me* [emphasis mine]... I had overlooked the fact that love might require something of me. I wanted [my husband] to make my well-being his highest priority, but I was unwilling to do the same for him.
>
> I was using my husband.
>
> It finally occurred to me that in spite of all my sophisticated education, I knew almost nothing about love.

I had overlooked the fact that love might require something of me. I was using my husband. It finally occurred to me that I knew almost nothing about love. Does any of this ring true for you? Are you serving, or loving, your husband the way you expect him to serve, or to love, you? If not, why not? Because if you're not serving your husband, that can only mean one thing: you don't know how to love.

Either that or you've stored up so much resentment over the years that it's getting in your way. Women are besieged with a myriad of thoughts and feelings on any given day, many of which are negative rather than positive. The trick is not to give them so much credit. Rather, determine which feelings matter and which ones don't. It's crucial that you do this because how we feel about something or someone at a particular moment in time doesn't necessarily mean anything. Feelings cannot be relied upon. But good sense can.

To move forward, start to put your feelings in perspective. If you're thinking negative thoughts about your husband or your marriage, it may in fact stem from something else. Maybe you're haunted by a past relationship that's getting intertwined with your current one. Or maybe something happened at work that's unrelated to your marriage but you've somehow made it about your marriage. Or perhaps your friend told you something about *her* marriage and now your head is swimming with thoughts about your own marriage. You must determine the source of your feelings so you don't assume you have a problem when you don't.

I'm not saying your feelings don't matter or that they're never an indication that something is awry. I'm saying to first figure out whether what you're feeling is "valid" or not. As females, we are walloped by so many emotions that it takes a great deal of discipline to push the ones away that don't need to be there. All they do is get you off track.

One way to gain perspective on your feelings is to spend time away from your husband. Silence and separation can be enormously instructive. When we're upset about something, resentment toward the person close to us is sometimes inevitable. And no one can serve someone they resent. It won't work.

If you are resentful toward your husband about something he did or about something you don't like about him, figure out what that it. Such resentments can be big, or they can be small things that over time ruffle feathers. For instance, Bill has a very annoying and almost constant habit of clearing his throat. He also doesn't wipe the counters or turn on the dishwasher when he's finished cleaning the kitchen. He gets in the shower ten minutes before we're supposed to be somewhere. He eats any food he finds, even if it's hidden, so I can never set anything aside just for myself that I know will be there a week later.

Those are small things, obviously. As for bigger resentments, here was the number one problem in our marriage for years: Bill and I both work from home. That is, until recently, we both worked from home—I now have an office. With the advent of mobile jobs, this is not an unusual problem for couples today; perhaps it works for some people. But in our case, the nature of what each of us does is very different.

As a writer, I need complete silence to get my work done. I cannot have any interruptions, which is why any writing I've done over the years has been when my kids were either asleep or in school. I've never tried to write actual content when my family is home. I can work on some things, but there's no way I could have written a book with children in my midst.

My husband's job is different. It requires him to move in and out of the house each day, often times vacillating between work and family tasks on any given week. I, on the other hand, am either working or running a household—there's no overlap. The result was that there were always interruptions. If my husband took a shower or even so much as went to the bathroom after I'd experience an hour or two of complete silence, it would interrupt my train of thought and I'd get angry. If he so much as knocked gently on the door to ask a question, I'd become enormously frustrated. I just can't be disturbed at all when I'm writing.

Now that I have an office outside the home, everything is a thousand times better. It was only then that I realized how much resentment I'd accrued over the years, which of course became directed toward my husband. And yet he wasn't doing anything wrong—it was just our circumstances. But I hated our circumstances! It was only once we changed them that the resentment I had disappeared. Loving Bill, or serving him, is so much easier now. Seeing him at the end of the day, rather than throughout the day, is awesome.

The task for you will be to determine what it is you resent and how you can remedy it. Your circumstances are not going to be mine, but it's important that you get to the bottom of it. Is your resentment something your husband can do something about? Is it something that's easily resolved, as mine was, or is it something bigger because it can't be changed? Before you can serve your husband, you have to figure this out.

If it's simply a matter of circumstances, then change the circumstances. If it's more severe than that, if it has to do with something your husband does that you don't like, or something about the way your husband behaves that you don't like, that will require something bigger of you (more on this in the next chapter). You can change your circumstances, but you can't change people. But from wherever the resentment stems, until you resolve it you will find it impossible to love, or to serve, your husband.

I'm sure your husband could come up with a laundry list of things about you that bother him. For instance, Bill hates it when we rake the leaves together because I rake them in piles and then leave them for him to put into bags. He also hates it when I don't clean the kitchen as I cook, the way he does, which makes the cleanup less daunting. Actually, he hates a lot of things I do. But as a man, he is *far less likely* than I am to store those feelings up as resentment. Rather, he accepts them.

You need to do the same, otherwise your relationship will be on unequal footing: your husband is overlooking your flaws and serving you anyway, but you're not reciprocating. Instead, you're absorbing every emotion and as a result are mired in resentment. That makes service impossible.

How do you change this rhythm? Don't attach so much significance to your feelings! If you're lonely or bored or frustrated or mad, don't assume your husband or the marriage is the problem. It's normal to feel those things. Don't assume you're no longer in love with your husband or that your husband doesn't know how to be married. Instead, let the feeling pass, swallow your pride, and do the very thing you don't feel like doing: serve.

Replace your feeling with an action.

If it helps, practice putting other people's needs ahead of your own *in general* so that service becomes part of your everyday life. I promise you will be a happier person. Because ultimately, happiness comes from giving, not getting.

One last thing. If you're worried about what other people think about the new you, don't be. Serving your husband has nothing to do with being a man's slave. That's just fear talking. If you want to turn things around in your marriage, if you want to make your marriage better, serve until it hurts. Serve until it feels like you're serving too much.

And then serve some more.

ACTION: For the next five days, focus on serving your husband. Make him a meal or a drink. Bring him the newspaper or a cup of coffee. Ask him if he needs anything. Listen without interjecting. Show respect, even if you think what he said is nuts. When you were dating your husband, you probably did all of these things happily. My guess is you stopped because resentment settled in. Don't let it.

6

HAVE ZERO EXPECTATIONS

What keeps many women from being willing to serve their husbands, aside from the resentment they harbor, are the expectations they have of marriage. High expectations are a major problem today, as women are encouraged to expect far more from men and marriage than any one person or institution can deliver.

When you enter a relationship with preconceived ideas about what should be or what can be, and things don't work out as planned, the only possible result is disappointment, which then fosters resentment. The only solution to this problem is to *dump your expectations altogether*. Obviously you expect your husband to be good to you and to be an active participant in the marriage; but barring such reasonable expectations, it's best to hope rather than to expect.

Men have far fewer expectations of marriage than women do. When men marry, they accept that what they see is what they get. They don't say "I do" thinking they're going to change or fix their wives later. Women, on the other hand, will actually marry a man they're not quite sure about, or who they think is "good enough," all the while thinking they can conform him into the man of their dreams. To illustrate the difference between men's and women's expectations of marriage, allow me to share a joke.

There's a store in New York City called The Husband Store, where women can go to choose a husband. At the entrance to the store is this sign: "You may visit the store ONLY ONCE!"

Inside, there are six floors; and the men's value increases as women ascend each flight of stairs. They are permitted to choose any man they want from a particular floor, or they can choose to go up another floor. They cannot, however, go back down except to exit the building.

So a woman goes into the store to find a husband. On the first floor the signs says, "These men have jobs." On the second floor, the sign says, "These men have jobs and love kids." On the third floor, the sign says, "These men have jobs, love kids, and are extremely good looking."

Wow, the woman thinks. This is great! Nevertheless, she keeps going. She goes to the fourth floor, and the sign there says, "These men have jobs, love kids, are drop-dead good looking, and help with the housework."

"Mercy me!" the woman says, "I can hardly stand it!" Yet still she goes up to the fifth floor. And the sign there reads, "These men have jobs, love kids, are drop-dead gorgeous, help with the housework, and have a strong romantic streak."

The woman is tempted to stop there, but she doesn't. Instead she goes to the sixth floor, where the sign reads, "You are visitor 3,261,496,012 to this floor. There are no men on this floor. This floor exists solely as proof that women are impossible to please. Thank you for shopping at The Husband Store."

To avoid gender bias charges, the store's owner opens The Wife Store just across the street. On the first floor are wives who love sex. On the second floor are wives who love sex and who are kind. On the third floor are wives who love sex, who are kind, and who enjoy sports.

The fourth, fifth, and sixth floors have never been visited.

Funny? Yes, because it's so true! Men, as a rule, are easy to please—which means by nature their expectations of marriage aren't high. Even if your husband does expect something, he's far more likely to hope you deliver than he is to demand you deliver. Men are practical too. They accept that when they make a decision, that's it—the decision is made. They don't fantasize about what could be or should be. They just live.

Women tend to believe there's a life they can live that will satisfy their every desire. But all choices, big and small, have trade-offs. Small: If you choose the steak, you can't have the fish. If you choose to go on the cruise, you can't get the house addition you wanted. Big: If you choose to marry a CEO or a brain surgeon, you have to accept that he'll rarely be home and you'll do all the work on the home front. Conversely, if you marry a family man you probably won't be rich.

Or here's a popular one: If you choose to make a career the center of your life and outsource your children's care, you'll have to accept the fallout of this lifestyle (which, for the record, is huge), as well as the guilt you'll feel for not being present on the home front. On the other hand, if you choose to make motherhood your primary job you will have less money in the bank.

Trade-offs are part of life. But women aren't encouraged to accept such trade-offs and as a result expect far too much from men and marriage. They focus on the "what-ifs" rather than on the what *is*. Let's look at three expectations about men and marriage many women harbor today.

#1 My husband should be my prince and my soul mate.

In the last chapter we talked about what love really is. Here's what it isn't: being swept away on a white horse by a gorgeous, svelte guy who makes a shit ton of money and who, miraculously, doesn't drink or gamble but is entirely selfless and is happy to hang out with his wife and kids and even do the dishes and the laundry. This. Man. Does. Not. Exist. (If he does, he's taken.) Many women say they know this is unrealistic, but they don't actually accept it. If they did, they wouldn't be so chronically dissatisfied.

And it's the culture that did it to them. By the time the average woman gets married, she's been drowning in "rom-coms," or romantic comedies. These films are meant to be an escape from real life, but rarely are women impervious to such stories. Women *feed* off romance—we love that stuff! But the message coming from Hollywood today is entirely unrealistic.

Did you know that in the past, Hollywood was bound by contract to produce films that were moral and practical in nature? There was still romance—in fact many would argue older films represent true romance—but Hollywood took its influence seriously and thus knew the messages they imparted could have real and lasting consequences. So they made films that were more in keeping with real life.

Take *Gone with the Wind*. In that film, the main character, Scarlett, is in love with Ashley. Ashley loves Scarlett too, but he's engaged to Melanie. Scarlett knows Ashley's engaged to Melanie, but Scarlett has no scruples, so she throws herself at Ashley every chance she gets. And while Ashley is hopelessly drawn to Scarlett, he refuses her advances and insists he's better suited to Melanie— even though Melanie doesn't light his fire the way Scarlett does. What's important, Ashley says, is honor. Here's the exchange between them:

Ashley: I'm going to marry Melanie.

Scarlett: But you can't, not if you care for me!

Ashley: Oh my dear, why must you make me say things that will hurt you? How can I make you understand? You're so young and unthinking, you don't know what marriage means.

Scarlett: I know I love you and I want to be your wife! You don't love Melanie!

Ashley: She's like me, Scarlett. She's part of my blood. We understand each other.

Scarlett: But you love *me*!

Ashley: How could I help loving you? You have all the passion for life that I lack. But that kind of love isn't enough to make a successful marriage for two people who are as different as we are.

I can't think of a single film in my lifetime that would dare to send a message like this one. On the contrary, Hollywood tells women that love conquers all. It sells the idea that women need only find their "soul mate" and everything will work out fine. That is a lie. You can be deeply in love with someone to whom you cannot be successfully married. (Trust me, I know *a lot* about that.)

Love wasn't even the original purpose of marriage. Marriage was initially about children and property. Even when love did become a focus, women had reasonable expectations as to what marriage could deliver. It wasn't until marriage became entirely optional, as a result of the Pill and of women's growing economic independence, that it began to shift from being about duty and obligation (combined with love) to being about finding a soul mate who can be everything you want all wrapped up in one man.

What a fruitless mission! So of all the millions of men in the world, a woman is supposed to find *this one man* who'll fulfill all her dreams and whose goals and personality mesh so beautifully with hers the two of them will never have to experience pain or disappointment again? If that's the plan going in, you're doomed.

The "soul mate" concept sets the bar too high. It's unsustainable.

In fact, romantic love is a lot like addiction. Tons of dopamine gets released in the early months or even years of a relationship, and it can make us downright stupid. You've heard the adage "love is blind"—that's where it comes from. But at some point that infatuation period ends, and the relationship shifts to a different stage of love. Or at least, that's the hope. And when that happens, people see their partners in a new light. When the initial phase of the relationship has passed, people realize they need a lot more than romance to keep it going. A *lot* more.

There is no man you can fall in love with for whom this will not be your fate.

At the end of the day, marriage is a much more pragmatic undertaking than women wish it was. In fact, life in general is a much more pragmatic undertaking than women wish it was. Life can't be endless parties and entertainment. If you chase that dream, you will be disappointed. The only way to make peace with marriage is to get comfortable with the mundane and find joy within that.

> Get comfortable with the mundane. If you're always seeking the next big thrill ride, you're destined to be unhappy.

#2 Marriage should be 50-50.

No expectation has been more damaging to women and to marriage than the feminist notion of equality. Notice I say the "feminist" notion. That's because a marriage *can* be equal, or equal enough, depending on how you define this term. So much of what is wrong with feminism has to do with the labeling. If you change the definition of a word or a phrase, the whole scenario looks different.

The equality you've been taught to embrace suggests men and women are interchangeable, and they are not. A marriage can be reasonably fair—I say "reasonably" because nothing in life is fair, to anyone—without both partners living identical lives.

Let's say you and I went into business together. To make it work, we would no doubt divvy up the tasks associated with the business. You'd be responsible, say, for the bookkeeping and for getting new clients, whereas I'd be responsible for working with those clients.

For the business to operate effectively, both of our tasks are equally important. Without one, we can't have the other. We are a team.

It's the same way in marriage. Raising a family requires a myriad of tasks that are impossible for one person to do alone successfully. If there's respect in the marriage, it shouldn't make any difference who's performing which task—assuming the tasks have been arranged according to what both people think is best. When you start playing tit for tat, which in practice is what feminism is about, your marriage is doomed.

The America of today wants you to believe that couples who both work full time and split household chores and childrearing right down the line have an "equal," and thus, forward-thinking, marriage. But this version of equality makes no allowances for sex differences. Being capable of doing the same things does not mean you both *want* to do the same things. And that's okay! You don't have to perform the same tasks in the same way at the same time to prove some faux notion of equality.

How much work you or your husband does on the homefront depends upon several factors, such as which one of you is home more. If I had been the full-time breadwinner and my husband had been home with our kids all these years, obviously he would have done more around the house than I would have. Whoever's home more is going to do more of the work at home.

When both partners work full-time and year-round, marriage has the potential to become a war zone. It's not a coincidence that as more and more women became breadwinners, we've heard more and more about who's doing what on the homefront. If both partners are leading identical lives, it's only natural to keep score.

When you read articles or when you hear news reports about how husbands and wives divvy up the breadwinning, childcare, and household chores, what you rarely hear is that most women do not work outside the home at the same rate as most men. This distinction is important because, as I said, whoever's home more is naturally going to do more of the work in that domain.

The notion that most women work the equivalent of two full-time jobs while men work only one job is a feminist fairy tale. The average woman in America works 26 hours per week outside the home, and the average man works 48. A study in the *Journal of Economic Literature* reports that while women perform roughly 17 more hours of work inside the home, men perform roughly 22 more hours outside the home. When comparing the total amount of work men and women each do *inside and outside the home*, women average 56 hours and men average 61.

My husband and I, for instance, may appear to be a two-income household—and on paper we are. But my husband is the steady earner. How much I "work" depends entirely on where my children are in their development, both physically and emotionally. When they were babies and toddlers, I dropped out of sight completely. When they're grown and gone, I expect to up the ante. In the meantime, it's hit or miss. That's a fair representation of most families today.

Those studies you read about also don't take into account the work your husband *does* do at home. They just hone in on the dishes and the diapers. What about the gutters and the garage? Or the lawn? What about all the things that need tending to outdoors or in the basement, like the plumbing or the roof? What about transporting the kids to and from school or sporting events? What about picking things up at the grocery store on the way home from work? These are things single guys don't do. They're things that come with the responsibility of being a husband and father, and most men live up to the task.

In other words, both partners today are working equally hard, just in different locales. This is true even for the unemployed mother who makes home and family her primary "job." Those women are managing the home and the family, and that is no small task. The more kids you have, the more taxing it is.

At the end of the day, it's about teamwork. If you choose to tally up a score, as the culture encourages you to do, you're destined to be miserable.

#3 My husband/marriage should make me happy.

Being happily married does not mean you're happy all the time. On any given day, week, month, or year you will not be happy— nor will you have warm fuzzies for your husband. In fact, there are times when your marriage may absolutely suck. So go with it—let it suck. The reason it sucks sometimes is because life sucks. Don't assume that whatever's happening means you married the wrong man or that your marriage is doomed. Don't assume that because things aren't working out the way you want them to at that particular moment in time that you need a different life.

If you're chronically unhappy, that *is* something to address. But if that's the case, it isn't necessarily your husband or the marriage that's causing your unhappiness. It could likely be something that rests within you. One of the reasons the rate of divorce in remarriages is astronomically high—70%!—is because women think a new man or a new life will bring them happiness. They also assume their ex was the problem when the problem may likely have been them.

This can be even be true if a woman's ex is a cad. Because the fact that she chose a man of that caliber in the first place speaks volumes about *her*. To find out why she made the choice she did, she should be focusing inward, not outward, to determine what she wants and what's keeping her from getting there. If a woman remarries without this knowledge in place, she will likely get divorced again.

A second divorce is even more likely when children are involved. A marriage with children involved bears no resemblance to a marriage without children. So much about marriage is about sacrificing one's needs for the sake of family. The happiness of each parent is not only secondary, it's irrelevant.

That may sound depressing at face value. But once you accept that marriage isn't designed to make you happy, it frees you up to focus on what *does* make you happy. By recognizing your happiness level begins and ends with you, your energy will be focused in the right direction.

Acceptance

Having zero expectations also makes it easier to become more accepting, which is critical for love to last. If you set the bar lower, you're much more likely to be able to live with whatever comes your way. Because if what happens is what you expected to happen, you're prepared. If it's better, great. If it's worse, well, you didn't fall that far from where you started.

Having expectations forces your marriage into a box. If the expectations don't fit, if that person or that thing doesn't do what you want, you're going to be miserable. That doesn't mean there's anything wrong with that person or that thing. It means you set things up to *make it seem* as though there's something wrong with that person or that thing.

There's a great saying that goes, "Life is what happens to you when you're busy making other plans." In other words, life is going to go the way it's going to go—there's only so much control you have. That's why you're much better off dumping your expectations altogether. Accept what is, and stop fighting what isn't. Take what comes your way.

When you accept something, no matter what it is, all of the sudden life looks different. Better. Easier. By having no expectations, you remove the inevitability of disappointment. And if you're not disappointed, there's nothing to be upset about. And if you're not upset, there's no reason for conflict!

I'll give you some really benign examples. Remember when I said Bill doesn't turn on the dishwasher or wipe the counters when he cleans the kitchen? I used to expect that he would do these things. I mean if you're going to clean the kitchen, you should clean it all the way. That's a reasonable expectation, right? But for whatever reason, he will clean an entire kitchen and leave crumbs all over the counter and not turn on the dishwasher. It made me nuts.

One day I just accepted that I'd be turning on the dishwasher and wiping the countertops every night for the rest of my life. I mentally incorporated that task into my list of things to do, and the result was a psychological shift of sorts. I no longer get upset because I have no expectation when I walk in the kitchen that those things will be done. If they are, great. But I don't expect it.

The alternative would be to nag, plead, or cajole my husband (and believe me, I tried them all) in the hopes that on some magical day, it would suddenly click for my husband, and he would say to himself, "Suzanne's right! This *is* how it should be done!" Alas, that never happened.

I think I also mentioned that Bill gets in the shower 10 minutes before we need to be somewhere or before company is due to arrive. For years, this made me crazy; and all my nagging and complaining was in vain. Finally, I accepted that this is what my husband does, and I can't change it. Rather than beat a dead horse, I decided to take a different approach. I matter-of-factly let Bill know—with no trace of anger or resentment—that I plan to drive myself to the event. I guess he didn't like that idea because he now gets in the shower much earlier.

> If we act "as if" something already exists, we set the stage for that thing, whatever it is, to manifest itself.

This is a great example of how the change you want to see may very likely occur when you accept certain things about your spouse and get creative about ways to work around those things. This removes the negative emotions that might otherwise emerge. In the past, Bill and I would fight constantly about when he planned to get in the shower. Now we don't.

Another option is to act "as if" your husband is the opposite of what he actually is (neat and tidy, punctual, well-mannered, etc.). It will require you to do some pretending, but that's okay. It works because your husband wants to make you happy, so if you assume the best—rather than point out the worst—he will likely rise to that assumption. As we learned in Chapter 2, the "law of attraction" means that if we act as though something already exists (whether it does or not), we set the stage for that thing, whatever it is, to manifest itself. You fake it 'til you make it, in other words.

There's one caveat, though. To be effective at acting "as if" (which essentially means you're ignoring your husband's flaws), you need to be open to the fact that whatever you wish your husband would do he won't necessarily do. He probably will, but he may not. Or he will, but it may take months or even years until he does. Either way, you have to be ready to love him even if he doesn't step up to the plate, otherwise he'll assume your love is conditional. And that will destroy any incentive he may have to improve.

I'll use a familiar example since I've already brought it up. The day I stopped paying attention to my husband's food and exercise regime, the day I acted as if Bill was already fit—or that he was capable of getting fit without my instruction—is the day he changed. Literally. He may not have gone out for a three-mile run at that very moment, but something within him shifted. I didn't see it at the time, but looking back I can see it clear as day. He was empowered almost immediately because he knew I was no longer looking over his shoulder telling him what he needed to do to get fit and has since taken it upon himself to make the necessary changes.

I also no longer tell him how to drive, and the result is the same. Acceptance is a much bigger problem for women than it is for men. Men aren't known for trying to change the woman they love—in fact some husbands hate the idea of their wives changing at all!—but women are notorious for trying to change their man. This is particularly true for alpha females, whose standards and expectations tend to be high. Alphas view imperfections as a challenge, something with which they feel they can *and should* improve upon. Accepting something in its flawed state is extremely difficult for the alpha female.

Can you see how this is a problem when you're married? Like you, your husband is flawed. But it isn't your job to fix him any more than it's his job to fix you. Your husband sees your flaws, but he accepts them. He doesn't dwell on them or try to figure out how he can get you to improve (unless he's a really high alpha, in which case he's probably an ass). Husbands do notice things, but they choose to overlook them. They accept things as they are, even if they don't like it. Wives need to do the same.

As an alpha female, I find acceptance very hard—even now. It's really hard for me to let things be less than I know they can be or to let other people figure things out for themselves when I know of something that can help them. For years I've been teaching or instructing in some capacity—with my students, in my teaching days; with my kids, as their mother; even as a writer. It was just natural for me to do the same with my husband. Plus it was the model I had growing up.

My mother instructed everyone in the family; that's just how it worked. And it's how it worked in *her* family. My mother's upbringing was very Victorian. Her grandmother, with whom she lived and who in fact raised my mother, was downright mean according to my cousin Ned, who also lived with their grandmother for a while. Whatever "flaws" my mother had as a child would not have been overlooked, of that I am confident.

Fortunately, my mother was a much softer person than the hard, dictatorial women in her family. But she was still an alpha and thus could not let go of her perfectionist ways. Any imperfection had to be recognized and improved upon in some way. My poor mother wouldn't have understood the concept of acceptance if you gave her an instruction booklet.

Needless to say, I absorbed some of this. I have very specific ideas about how I want to live, and assumed Bill would, and should, join me for the ride. It was a two-fer! Whatever I decided was the "right" way to live was the way he should live, too. After all, we're married. So I took that to mean we should live identical lives.

But that doesn't take into account two things. One, that men and women are different; and two, that my husband has an identity of his own, separate from mine. It is therefore unreasonable for me to expect him to live a life *I've* designed for him.

It is no small thing when a wife does not accept her husband as he is, or when he feels she doesn't accept him. If you don't accept your husband, or if he feels you don't, he assumes your dissatisfaction means you think you made a mistake in marrying him. (His brain: Why did she marry me if she didn't like what she saw?)

In addition, a husband's view of himself is influenced by his wife's view of him. So if you think little of him, he'll think little of himself. If you think he's the berries, he'll believe that too. Then he'll become the berries! See how it works? As always, it begins with you.

> The husband of a woman's imagination is always better than the husband she actually has.

Finally, by not accepting your husband you essentially have one foot out the door at all times. Because when you concentrate on the ways in which your husband is lacking, you naturally think about other men. A husband doesn't fantasize about life with another woman every time his marriage hits a snag. That survey I mentioned in Chapter 2 about the 50% of married women who had a backup husband? Those would not be the results if married men had been polled. That's not how men think.

The husband of a woman's imagination is always better than the husband she actually has. I know a woman who was involved in an affair for no other reason than she was bored with her perfectly wonderful husband. They got divorced as a result, and of course her affair didn't last. Several years later, the woman realized how great her first husband is; and fortunately for her, he took her back.

I don't know whether that was a good move or a bad move on the husband's part, but the point is still the same. By focusing on what her husband was lacking, whatever it was, this woman set up a false reality and got burned. She simply lucked out—most men would not have taken their ex-wife back.

ACTION: Dump your expectations of marriage, and accept your husband as he is right now. Make a list of the things in life you absolutely must have to be content—money, food, shelter, love, loyalty, trust, etc.—and if you have them, be satisfied. Act "as if" your husband is the man of your dreams and see if he becomes just that.

7

DON'T USE MONEY AS A WEAPON

Who makes the decisions in your household when it comes to the big-ticket items? When you and your husband disagree on a house project—whether or not to do it, or when to do it, or which one to do—or when the two of you disagree about where to go on vacation, who casts the deciding vote? How you answer this question determines who holds the power in the relationship.

Who's in charge of the checking account matters too. Because that person has control over discretionary spending, and discretionary spending is what causes conflict. No one fights over the bills that have to get paid. The person who's in charge of the checking account is the same person who sees how the money is being spent, which means the person who's not in charge of the checking account is at the mercy of bill payer. The bill payer may not be *trying* to control the other person's spending; but he or she has the advantage of seeing what's moving in and out of the account, so it's inevitable. Later in the chapter I offer a solution to this problem.

If it happens that the breadwinner in your marriage is also the person who pays the bills, that person has all the power in the relationship. But if the breadwinner allows the other person to control the daily spending, the power is more equally distributed.

This may come as a surprise (since the culture tells you otherwise), but in the past financial power *was* evenly distributed in many, if not most, households. As the breadwinners, men may have had control over big-ticket items, but wives typically maintained control of the family's day-to-day spending. "Even if a woman does not earn a paycheck, she is likely the gatekeeper to her household's expenditures," writes Bridget Brennan, author of *Why She Buys*.[1]

> A man's need to provide for his family is integral to his very being—it is never good news if a wife usurps that role.

This is true today, and it was true in our mothers' day. Yes, there were husbands who did not allow their wives any control over the spending. But there's no reason to assume that was the norm. And some of those husbands may have been justified if their wives were chronic overspenders.

Today, things have changed. Most women bring home a paycheck of some sort, which alters the dynamic considerably. The culture hails women's newfound earning power as a great thing, a boon for women and for society. And it may be. But depending on how a woman handles these circumstances, it can be very bad news for her marriage.

A man's need to provide for his family is integral to his very being—it is never good news if a wife usurps that role. Men in America are effectively being de-programmed to be something different from what nature dictates, and fighting human nature never ends well. It's hardly a coincidence that the divorce rate skyrocketed as more and more women became breadwinners. Nor is it a coincidence that wives are the ones who file for divorce most often.

They're using money as a weapon.

Let's face it: money is power. That's why it causes so much conflict in marriage. How much conflict it causes depends on a host of factors, the most significant being the quality of the relationship and the attitude each partner has toward money. Each of us carries with us a mindset about money. As children, we watched our parents muddle through the maze of shared finances and came away with certain beliefs as a result. Whatever values, or whatever verbal or nonverbal messages, our parents sent about money ultimately formed our views.

If the arguments your parents had about money revolved around not having enough, the takeaway might have been that wealth is a panacea for marital conflict. (If only!) If the arguments your parents had about money revolved around control—one person had it, and the other didn't—the takeaway might have been that money can (or should) be used as a means of control. If there were zero arguments about money in your household, congratulations. You've just qualified for the *Guinness Book of World Records*.

Many women (and men, for that matter) become alphas as a result of the messages they absorbed about money as a child. Remember Anna in *Leap Year*? The one whose father couldn't hold a job, which led to so much financial upheaval her family home was repossessed? I'm convinced that's what happened with my mother, only the story is somewhat different.

My mother's father could certainly hold a job—and did. He was an engineer and salesman of industrial equipment for Westinghouse. Unfortunately, he was laid off in 1932 during the Great Depression and did not find permanent work until World War II. As a result, for the first ten years of my mother's life, her father was home and unemployed. He spent that time inventing a rotary engine for trains, which he ultimately patented. (Years after the patent expired, a Japanese automaker developed a car engine based on that patent.)

When he lost his job, my grandmother, who had a college degree (yes, it was possible for women in the early twentieth century to get college degrees), became the family breadwinner. She established, and then managed, the library at the St. Louis Art Museum, and that job kept the family afloat. Still, they never owned a home. Three generations lived in a small, three-bedroom apartment with one bathroom and no air-conditioning. At one point they had to move to California to live with an uncle. No one in the family owned a car, either. My mother's primary mode of transportation was either her bicycle or the streetcar.

These experiences had a huge effect on my mother. Throughout her life, money represented one thing only: security. Since the person who was "supposed" to take care of her financially was unable to do so, and since she was raised in an era of financial uncertainty, she had a very hard time trusting others to be in charge of anything, let alone money. When she later inherited some money in her forties from the uncle in California (who had no children), she held on to it for dear life. That money became her lifeblood. It was hers and hers alone.

My father, an accountant, took care of our family's finances. But my mother never pooled my father's income with the funds she received from her uncle; many women who inherit money keep ownership of that money, particularly in the past when women weren't typically employed. Even today, inherited money is not considered marital property. This might have been okay, theoretically—if she had not used the money as a means of control.

But here's the thing: she wasn't trying to control my father—she was trying to keep control of her life. Either way, though, the result is the same. When you keep separate accounts that limit the other person's access or power, you undermine the marriage. Because what you're basically saying is, "I don't trust you."

Fortunately, as I wrote in the introduction, my father understood my mother and thus cut her a lot of slack. He knew her trust issues were deeply rooted. He was also the sole breadwinner and gave my mother a weekly cash "allowance," which she had no problem with since she was extremely frugal and didn't spend much money anyway. Plus, if she really wanted to buy something, she had the funds to do so.

In fact, my mother's frugality was the biggest problem in their marriage. That might sound odd, or even heavenly, to someone who's married to a spendthrift, but my mother was actually worse than frugal. She was an "underspender."

No, really, that's a thing. My mother was literally petrified to spend a dime, so that's what most of my parents' fights were about:

the fact that my mother *couldn't* spend money. Here are the signs of an underspender:

- Having an adequate amount of savings and income and still worrying about money regularly

- Not seeking basic healthcare because you're afraid of the costs

- Ignoring fixable problems because you don't think they're worth the money to repair

- Feeling physical pain or anxiety when spending any amount of money

- Refusing to throw away any amount of food, no matter how small

- Continuing to use broken or worn out items

- Constantly justifying your lack of spending with the mantra "I might need it someday"

- Avoiding all investment vehicles that come with any sort of risk

If my father were alive today, he would look at that list and shake his head. That is *precisely* what his life with my mother was like—it was not fun. One of the most frustrating aspects of my mother's frugality was her tendency to hoard. My parents owned one home throughout their entire marriage, and my mother could not throw anything away—not even a three-year-old piece of aluminum foil. For years my father begged my mother to clean out the basement, but he was never successful in his mission.

So that was my story. Yours is different, I'm sure. Regardless, we all come away from our upbringing with an understanding that money is about security, power, or control. Or some combination thereof.

Back in the days before most women began earning their own money, wives were obviously dependent on their husbands' incomes. The culture would have you believe this was because women were oppressed, but there's a perfectly good reason why women were dependent on men. It's called children.

It's hard to imagine now, but there was a time when simply getting married, for a woman, meant a gaggle of kids and lifetime of housework and child care. There was no way around it for women who lived prior to the invention of the Pill (or the countless other birth control methods we have today). But just because women now have the choice to control the size of their families, and thus the direction their lives will take, doesn't mean they don't still want family to be their primary focus.

Most mothers do not work full-time and year-round, which means most married women are still financially dependent upon a husband for a specified amount of time. The only wives for whom this does not apply are those who choose not to have children or those who never stay home with their children for more than the allotted six- or twelve-week maternity leave period. But that group, contrary to what the media would have you believe, isn't the norm.

The obvious advantage of depending on a husband's income for a period of time, aside from being able to stay home with one's babies, is that husbands feel needed—and this has a positive effect on the marriage. You may hear a lot about how men feel "burdened" being the sole breadwinner, but that's just feminist gobbledygook. (And for the record, feminists are *the last people on earth* who should be dispensing advice on men and marriage.) The research shows, and biology dictates, that men view breadwinning as their responsibility.

> Societal changes do not eradicate biological leanings.

Husbands may lament the pressures they face at work, but that doesn't mean they don't want the pressure. Most men use such pressure to help propel them forward. That's why married men fare better financially than single men. Marriage acts as a stabilizer for men: they become motivated toward success when their families are depending on them. It's true that a husband may like the extra income his wife brings home, and these days may even encourage his wife to work outside the home due to the high cost of living (a direct result of the two-income family), but most men have no desire to *rely* on their wives' incomes.

Societal changes do not eradicate biological leanings. Men want to protect and provide for their families because it is in their nature to do so. When a (good) man's wife is counting on him in this way, her respect for him comes naturally. When a wife makes an equal or greater income, the game changes. The wife knows she doesn't "need" her husband, and over time she becomes more and more alpha. Then she officially usurps her husband's role.

That's why men tend to marry "down": there's no competition. It's also the reason successful women often wind up alone. Think of all the really powerful women you know of. Now count how many are married.

I'm not writing this with any judgment on the matter. I didn't say it was fair or that it's as it should be. It just is. It isn't new, either. It has been this way since the dawn of the ages, and it isn't likely to change anytime soon. "In 2001, wives earned more than their spouses in almost a third of married households where the wife worked. Yet this proud professional achievement often seems to have unhappy consequences at home."[2]

Now for the million-dollar question: Am I suggesting we go back to the 1950s, when most women were supported financially by their husbands?

The short answer is no, we could never go back, even if we wanted to. But don't be quick to assume women today have it so much better than women did "back in the day." Remember, women robbed Peter to pay Paul: they may be financially independent, but they're also exhausted and angry. And if they have children, they're saddled with guilt and stress—two words women back in the day never used to describe their lives.

The question isn't "Do we go back?" It's "How do we move forward?" How can women be independent earners if they choose to and still be happily married? *By leaving the power thing at the door*. Walk out of your house an alpha, but come back a beta.

It's also smart to keep your career choice simple. Choose a profession you can do part time or that allows for flexibility. Because the bigger your job is, the more you're going to struggle on the home front, both in your marriage and with your kids.

If that advice offends you, it should tell you something: that you've placed far too much significance on what you do and not enough on who you are and who you love. Because at the end of the day, the latter is what matters most.

As former Wall Street hot shot-turned wife and mother Erin Callen Montella wrote in *Full Circle*, "Don't forsake relationships and family and children for your job. It's not worth it. It will never be worth it. It will inevitably end in disappointment. It has to. Keep those priorities in the forefront as you try to live a happy and productive life. Make choices that are consistent with those priorities. Pursue career paths that allow for the roles you want those priorities to play in your life."[3]

At the end of the day, we can choose power or love. Rarely do the two go together—for anyone. A high alpha male is just as unlikely as a high alpha female to have a great marriage because they're both consumed with power. And the more powerful you become, the less stable your marriage will be. Marriage requires attention. If you're not home long enough to feed the relationship, if you're inattentive or otherwise distracted, the marriage will die.

Some women have the good sense to recognize this in advance. Oprah Winfrey is famous for saying she never married or had kids because she knew ahead of time what kind of life she wanted, and it wouldn't be fair to pursue that life as a wife and mother. And when Katharine Hepburn was asked by *Ladies' Home Journal* why she never had children, she said, "Well, I'm not dumb enough to think I could have handled that situation. If your mind is on something else, you are useless. If someone needs you, they need YOU! That's why I think women have to choose. I remember making the decision to never marry and have children. I want to be a star, and I don't want to make my husband and children my victims.'"[4]

Fortunately, most of us don't have to choose between being a famous actress or television personality and being a good wife. Most of us can be married and still have careers, but the bigger those careers are, the harder it will be to stay married. At some point along the line, you'll be force to choose between power and love and will likely end up using your income as a weapon. Why do you think most Hollywood marriages fail?

I'm not suggesting women not pursue those big careers—I'm simply pointing out the risks they take in choosing to do so. It is not an accident that so many highly successful women are single or divorced.

I know it's trendy to encourage girls to become surgeons, CEOs, or even the President, but I would no more advise my daughter to do that than I would my son. I don't want either of my kids to choose careers that will consume their lives. I believe a simple life focused on family brings the greatest joy in life. And no matter how great a person's professional accomplishments may be, they won't mean a thing if his or her home life is a mess.

Success has a serious price tag. Several years ago I watched a documentary on the band Journey. In it, Ross Valory, one of the band members, reminisced about the early days of the band's success. Here's what he had to say: "A lot of people don't know what the price is when they step up to the plate. The wear and tear is a mental and emotional thing. You really just let go of a lot of relationships that require presence and constant nurturing. You say good-bye to people. People get sick and die when you're gone, and just a lot of things go by the wayside."[5]

At that point in the interview Valory began to tear up. In fact, several of the band's members—including Steve Perry, the lead singer, and guitarist Neil Schon, who's been married five times—

have talked openly about how success destroys love. They even convey this message in their songs.

Another reason to keep your career choice simple, aside from it giving your marriage a boost, is that women who make more than their husbands are no happier about it than men are! *Forbes* staff writer Michael Noer took a lot of heat for making this point in his 2006 article, "Don't Marry Career Women." In it, Noer highlighted research that found *both* men and women are unhappy when wives make more money than their husbands. "A recent study in *Social Forces* found that women—even those with a feminist outlook— are happier when their husband is the primary breadwinner," he wrote.[6]

No matter how great a person's professional accomplishments may be, they won't mean a thing if his or her home life is a mess.

Anthropology professor John Townsend published similar findings in *What Women Want—What Men Want*. After completing a copious amount of research on gender preferences and the effect of employment on marriage, Townsend himself was surprised to learn (having grown up in the heyday of feminism) that "the potential for conflict in equal-partner marriages is very great."[7]

That isn't surprising. The stress level in marriages in which both parents work full time and year-round is off the charts. When two people are trying to perform the same tasks, of course there's more potential for disagreement. If neither partner is considered "in charge" of a particular task, there will be constant negotiation going on that would otherwise not occur if each person had designated tasks.

Even in marriages where the husband stays home and the wife works, women are ambivalent about this role reversal. Such relationships tend to follow the same pattern: the wife loses respect for her husband; he feels emasculated, and then the sex stops.

Biology matters. Most women are not sexually attracted to a man who doesn't earn a living or who makes considerably less than she does. Are there couples that reverse these roles and manage to make it work? Yes. But they're the exception, not the rule.

Men and women may both be capable of being breadwinners or full-time parents, but that doesn't mean they both want to do those tasks with equal fervor. More often than not, a man's identity is inextricably linked to his paycheck, and a woman's identity is linked to her children. That this does not hold true for every woman and every man doesn't change the fact that what drives most women is different from what drives most men.

Think of it this way. You, as a female, are able to do something no man can: give birth. What on earth can top that? Nothing—it's miraculous. And men don't have this power. I'm not saying men secretly long to give birth. I'm saying a man's ability to provide for the family he's created is integral to his identity. That's something he *can* do.

For women, the ability to give birth is integral to *their* identity. Any gynecologist can tell you that most women, if they haven't had children by their mid-thirties, become anxious. They cannot envision a life without children. No matter how committed they may be to their jobs, that desire is there. And when it's met, the woman's nurturing gene kicks in. Providing for that child emotionally, not financially, will be her first instinct.

A man's first instinct is to make money, and his career is his means to do that. It's his unparalleled accomplishment in the same way giving birth is to you. When a man isn't providing for his family in a manner he deems satisfactory—meaning, if he doesn't make enough money, or if you make more money than he does, or if you spend more than he's able to earn—he will not be happy. If by some miracle your husband could give birth tomorrow, wouldn't that take something away from you?

It is a fact of human nature, grounded in evolutionary biology, that women prefer to marry men who make more money than they do. There's even a name for it: hypergamy. The average single woman doesn't cue in on a man's earning power because of greed. She does so because somewhere in the back of her mind, no matter what her career plans may be, she wants the option to stay home with her babies. And the only way to do that is to have a breadwinning husband.

> The happiest marriages are those that are more traditional in nature. This does not mean the wife never works outside the home or that the husband isn't an engaged father. It just means the husband makes a larger income. When he does, both partners are happier.

This is a perfectly reasonable—indeed, smart—attitude for a woman to have. When I first met my husband, he was on a steady career track. But several years prior to that, he'd been floundering after receiving two higher degrees. He was working at the Washington University library, making very little money. He may have had a great education and a job with some measure of cache, but I had no qualms telling him after we met that I would not have gone out with him had I met him several years earlier. He did not take offense to this, for he noticed when he was working at the library that when he would meet a woman and tell her what he did for a living, she lost interest. Only then did he get serious about his career goals. Several years later, he and I met.

Unfortunately, the culture we live in today encourages women to ignore a man's salary because a woman is supposed to take care of herself. But getting a good education and developing a skill for the marketplace, which every woman (and man) should do, does not supplant maternal desire. Most women have children, even if they put it off. And when they do, they won't have the option to stay home unless they chose a man who's a steady earner or who was in a position to become a steady earner. Nor will they have this option if they made financial decisions based on two incomes instead of one; or if they ignored, or more likely didn't know because no one told them, the psychological toll their financial success would have on their marriage.

Take Karie's story. Here's what she conveyed to me in an email:

When I was growing up, my mother stressed the importance of getting a good career as a woman. Her father, my grandfather, had died when my mom was in her teens and left my grandmother with nothing. The family struggled. My mother never forgot the experience and strongly encouraged us children to become independent in all ways. I believed this message. It seemed sensible to me to be able to take care of myself.

Today I am 40 years old, and I make $350,000 per year as a physician. My husband works at home on our farm. It may sound like an ideal situation, but this role reversal has caused enormous conflict. I am jealous of the fact that he gets to stay at home, and he is jealous of the fact that I get to go to work. I lack respect for him because I'm bringing home all the money.

I regret that I'm not an at-home mom and wife, supporting my family instead of leading them. I leave the house at 4:30 am and get home at 6:30 pm. I am too tired for sex at night. My husband tries to lead, but I take charge because I am the breadwinner. When a woman is the breadwinner, she feels it is her right to lead the family.

The feminist message is so strong. We are all influenced by it. It is not good. It is not right.

Karie's story represents why, statistically speaking, the happiest marriages are those that are more traditional in nature. This does *not* mean a wife never works outside the home, nor does it mean a husband isn't an engaged father. It just means the husband makes the bulk of the income.

Stress and jealousy are the biggest factors that upset the equilibrium of marriages when the husband is out-earned by his wife. If the gender roles in Karie's marriage were reversed, if she was home and her husband was the physician, he would not be plagued with the feelings his wife has about the arrangement. If he had been the physician and Karie had stayed home, they'd be swimming with the tide rather than against it.

Accepting the reality of male and female nature doesn't mean wives (necessarily) need to quit their jobs or make a career change. But it does mean that women who have their own money need to be aware of how it affects their marriage, rather than assume it's no big deal. How sensitive a woman is to this power dynamic can make or break the marriage.

Joint Bank Accounts

None of this is to suggest that having a traditional marriage, one in which the wife is at home with the kids and may or may not be employed part time, ensures marital peace. But statistically, these couples do fare better, if for no other reason than because the variables discussed above have been eliminated. But regardless of who brings what to the table, one thing is certain: you must have joint bank accounts.

Many lawyers and psychologists recommend the opposite. That's because they spend their days with unhappy couples who are sticking it to each other financially. To prevent this from happening, they will suggest couples keep their monies separate. But I believe this attitude can work in reverse. Keeping money separate in the event of a divorce can in fact precipitate a divorce! And self-fulfilling prophecies are a thing I try to avoid.

When we marry, nothing is ever really our own anymore. That's why so many people delay marriage in the first place. It's hard to go from "mine" to "ours." But that's what marriage is. Everything is designed to become a joint effort. It shouldn't matter who performs which tasks—all the money should go into the same pot.

To be clear, I'm not suggesting you and your husband share a singular account and communicate at all times about every dollar spent. That isn't realistic. What I'm saying is that all money that comes into your household should be viewed as marital property. Where the money came from, or to whom the check is addressed, should be irrelevant. This not only builds trust, it allows for complete transparency. With the exception of petty cash for incidentals, you and your husband should know where most of the money is going at all times.

There's also the matter of who manages the checking account. If that person is you, *you need to be aware of the power this affords you.* Your husband doesn't want to feel like a child asking his mother for money any more than you would if he were the one managing the account, so it's important you set up a system where the person who doesn't pay the bills has some measure of power.

One way to do this is to use cash. In other words, whoever doesn't pay the bills would take out a certain amount of cash every week (or every two weeks, or every month) and be liberal with that amount so he or she ends up with extra cash. That keeps this person from having to ask the money manager if there's enough money in the bank for that person to use. Plus there's no paper trail, as there is with a shared debit card, which means when that person wants to buy coffee at Starbucks and not get grief about it, he or she has that option.

Another possibility is to have two joint checking accounts with debit cards: one the bill payer uses for monthly spending and for discretionary spending, and one the other person uses for his or her own discretionary spending. That second account would have an allotted, agreed upon amount dropped into it each pay period. This is the same plan as the cash idea, only the person would use a debit card instead.

Either system allows each partner some measure of control. It isn't healthy for one partner to have to ask the other if he or she can buy something minor (naturally, what constitutes "minor" depends on your household income), but it's especially bad for a husband to have to check with his wife. Nothing will kill his libido, and yours, faster.

> Regardless of who makes the money and who does the banking, it is imperative you have joint bank accounts.

If you're an alpha wife, you probably pay the bills. But be careful, and pay close attention to how it's affecting your marriage. If you're the breadwinner *and* you pay the bills, I can almost guarantee you're headed for disaster. If you're not employed, or if you work part time and your husband is the primary breadwinner, as long as you have a system in which your husband doesn't have to ask you for money you should be good to go.

If you are the sole or main breadwinner in your family, there's no getting around the fact that this is dangerous territory. To keep it from undermining your marriage, I would encourage you to let your husband manage the household finances, just as men typically have their wives do in more traditional marriages. If your husband has repeatedly proven himself to be careless with money, this may not be an option.

On the other hand, if you're simply assuming he isn't capable, or even if he agrees he isn't capable, it's possible you're both just used to your handling the finances and are afraid of what switching things up will mean for your marriage. At the very least, you'll find out whether what you believe to be true is in fact true.

I know you want to control the spending. I know you can't imagine trusting your husband with that job, but isn't that exactly what he's doing right now? Trusting you? If you cannot reciprocate, don't think for a moment this isn't a problem. It is. It means your husband trusts you, but you don't trust him. And that will manifest itself in a thousand different ways.

Discretionary spending is only part of the equation. There are also the big-ticket items, which should always be discussed between husband and wife. The problem, of course, is that someone needs to have the final say on those purchases because you both won't always agree. In many households, the person who has the final say tends to be the person who brings the most money to the marriage.

If your husband brings home the bulk of the income, he's probably the one who determines whether or not you both can afford that house addition or that vacation. If you bring home the bulk of the income, you're probably the one who makes those decisions. To which I'd say again: be careful. This arrangement is affecting your husband's psyche whether he's telling you it is or not.

If this *is* the arrangement in your household, you need to put the power back in your husband's hands. You can do this in several ways. One, turn your paycheck over to him to manage. Two, restructure your life so you're not the one bringing the most money to the table. (This could require a job change, a career change or simply cutting back your work hours.) Three, put your income aside in a joint savings account and live as much as possible on your husband's income (assuming he makes a reasonable salary). Or four, listen to your husband about the big-ticket items and do what he suggests is best.

If he wants to save more money for retirement and you want a house addition, don't overrule his decision or cajole him in such a way that you end up getting what you want. Instead, give up the idea of a house addition for the time being and save for retirement instead. This will be very difficult for the alpha wife to do (more on this in the next chapter), but it will come back to her in spades.

I know these are all big changes, and I can't make you do them. But I can give you these questions to think about:

1. Do you and your husband fight daily or even weekly about how to spend money?

2. Is your husband acting out in any way? Does he drink a lot? Retreat to the basement?

3. Does your husband feel as though you're his mother rather than his wife?

4. Does your husband initiate sex?

5. Does he take you out on dates?

How you answer these questions will determine how much of a problem money is in your marriage. Ideally, you want your answers to be: no, no, no, yes and yes. The further away you are from those answers, the more work you have to do. If you do not make serious changes, the marriage you have now is the marriage you will have for life.

Is it the one you want?

ACTION: If all your bank accounts are not joint, make them joint. Then, equalize the power by making sure the person who does not bring home the bulk of the income has decision-making power over discretionary items. Because if you bring home most of the income *and* you control all the finances, your marriage is a ticking time bomb.

8

STOP SAYING NO

Of all the proactive measures I've taken to bring about a more peaceful marriage, hands down my willingness to agree with my husband, as opposed to fighting with him and saying no all the time, has had the most powerful impact. I cannot tell you how many times Bill has asked me over the years, begged me really, to just say, "Okay."

My natural tendency is to either say no, or to offer an alternative, or to give my opinion, or to simply share what I think. I am 100% honest and 100% outspoken, which is both a blessing and a curse. In my professional life, telling the no-holds-barred truth is my brand. It's what I do. But I've learned that people only want honesty to a certain extent. Most of the time, when people seek advice, or when they say they want advice, that isn't true. Most of the time they just want the other person to agree with them.

This can be tricky in a marriage. Ideally, I'd like to think I can be my natural self at all times and my husband won't mind. In fact, I used to insist upon it. But there's something husbands crave more than truth: acceptance. Your husband wants you to accept his ideas almost as much as he wants to see you happy. And he doesn't want your opinion nearly as much as he wants your sympathy. "Three-fourths of the people you ever meet are hungry and thirsty for sympathy. Give it to them, and they will love you," writes Carnegie.[1]

If this is true, and I believe it is, I'm convinced I'm part of the 25% that doesn't look for sympathy from people. When I seek advice, or when I want to know what someone thinks, or when I make a statement about what I think, I *genuinely want to know* what the other person thinks. It doesn't matter to me whether it matches what I think, and I don't mind having my ideas challenged. This works well for me as a writer since my work is controversial, and being challenged is par for the course. If sympathy were my goal, I'm in the wrong profession.

What I've learned the hard way, though, is that Carnegie is right: most people don't operate that way (which is why most people don't do what I do!) And it is definitely *not* the way most husbands operate. When your husband comes to you with a problem, he wants you to listen to him, not to play devil's advocate. Telling your husband you don't agree with him is effectively telling him that his judgment is poor, and his reaction will be to retaliate. I never thought of it this way because, to me, debate comes naturally.

So does compartmentalization: I can separate the personal from the political very well. I can "duke it out," so to speak, with just about anyone—and then hug the person when it's over. No hard feelings. But most people do not enjoy doing battle, particularly with the people they love. So on the home front, I had no choice but to shift gears. I had to stop making every exchange with my husband into a battle.

Today I acquiesce. I say "okay" or "that's fine" or "I agree" or some other version of yes. My goal is to say yes as often as I can when communicating with my husband, and the result has been amazing. There is quiet where there used to be noise. There is peace where there used to be conflict.

Here's an example of what a typical conversation with my husband used to look like:

Him: I think we should buy more life insurance.

Me: What? We pay enough insurance as it is!

Him: Yes, but I'm concerned that if something happens to me, you won't have enough to tide you over until you get on your feet.

Me: The amount we have is fine.

Him: Well, I don't feel good about it. I'll feel better knowing you're taken care of.

Me: I'm sick of insurance companies taking everyone's money. People rarely collect. The whole thing's a scam.

Today, that same conversation looks like this:

Him: I think we should buy more life insurance.

Me: That's a great idea. Thank you for taking care of me.

Here's another example. I used to make all the arrangements for the dates my husband and I went on. I did it mainly out of habit but also because I like to know where I'm going, and I like to go where I want to go. My husband got so used to my taking over that he stopped taking the initiative. And if he did take the initiative, I likely had an opinion about it. I would often suggest we go to a place different from the one he suggested.

This is very common in marriage. Just today I read an online comment from a wife who said this about herself: "When my husband asks me where I want to eat, I always say, 'somewhere good.' And then reject every single one of his suggestions. I'm a delight."

What do you think happens in a marriage like that? The husband gives up, of course.

But I got tired of feeling like I was taking my husband out. Bill was essentially accompanying *me* on a date *I'd* arranged, which is not at all how our relationship began. (I'm sure that's not how yours did, either.) In those days, Bill made the first move, and I would follow. I wanted to get that dynamic back, so one day I decided to stop taking charge of our dates. Here's an example of a conversation between us then and now.

Then:

> Him: I made a reservation at Bar La Frere for Friday night.

> Me: Oh, wouldn't you rather go to Cardwell's? (Translation: I don't like your idea.)

Now:

> Him: I made a reservation at Bar La Frere for Friday night.

> Me: Sounds great!

Choosing not to argue with your husband is about understanding two things: male nature and human nature. Men don't like to fight with their wives, and people in general don't respond well to the word "no." "When a person says no and really means it," writes Carnegie, "he or she is doing far more than saying a word of two letters. The entire organism—glandular, nervous, muscular—gathers itself together into a condition of rejection. When, to the contrary, a person says 'Yes,' none of the withdrawal activities takes place. The organism is a forward-removing, accepting, open attitude."[2]

The more we say yes instead of no, the more we allow the other person to be open to what we think and to what we want. The problem for alpha wives is that saying "no" comes naturally. So does the temptation to tell someone he or she is wrong. But this is the wrong approach—see what I mean?—to take with your husband.

Same goes for interrupting, which was another challenge of mine. (As it happens, interrupting is something my husband does as well; but it's likely his behavior is a result of my behavior. I modeled it, and he adopted it.) I don't interrupt to be rude. I do it because Bill and I are usually short on time, and I feel we have to hurry up and get the conversation in before we're interrupted. Or I do it because I'm afraid I won't remember to come back to whatever it was he said with my own response. Nevertheless, the result is the same as if I interrupted to be rude.

Today I no longer engage in conversation when the clock is ticking. I wait until we have the time to give the matter our full attention. I've also come to accept that I don't need to make a counterpoint to every statement my husband makes. That's a debate, not a conversation. What my husband wants more than anything is to be heard. And if I'm interrupting, I'm not listening.

Another way wives go into fight mode with their husbands is by not taking no for an answer. When there's a disagreement of any sort, alpha females rarely capitulate—often because they're used to calling the shots or they're used to doing things their way in their day job. This was a big one for me. Since I've been home with my kids all these years, and since I'm self-employed, I haven't had a boss in ages. And those who don't have a boss aren't used to taking orders or to following someone else's plan of action.

That's one of the reasons I believe at-home mothers are particularly susceptible to becoming alpha wives. It's hard to switch from mother mode to wife mode. For years I've either been in charge of my kids or I've been in charge of my work. I make every decision there is to be made. So when Bill disagreed with me, it's uncomfortable.

It wasn't that I insisted on having my way in a childish or disrespectful manner. I never made decisions without Bill, and I didn't say, "This is how it's going to be, and you're just going to have to deal with it!" I would never talk to him that way. But what I did do was just as exasperating.

I wouldn't let up.

I'd carry on with something over and over again until I wore Bill down and got my way, which isn't hard for a woman to do since husbands long to please their wives. Your husband wants to see you happy, so he will ultimately surrender—even if he hates your idea.

But just because it's in your husband's nature to do that doesn't mean you should take advantage of it. When you do, in effect you're using your husband. Instead of respecting his feelings, you're using your feminine power to undermine your husband's ideas or judgment. That may get you what you want; but each time it happens, you're wearing away your husband's love for you bit by bit.

For years I wasn't even aware this dynamic existed in my marriage. I was just being me! I've always been persistent, and again, this trait has worked well for me in the professional sphere. But it's a perfect example of this book's theme: the qualities one needs to get ahead at work are the exact same qualities that will screw up your marriage. If you want to be successful in love, you need a whole new set of tools with which to work.

It's a mental shift that takes time and maturity to adopt. My propensity to say no is far greater than my propensity to say yes. (Just ask my kids.) And while saying "no" is part and parcel of being a mother, it is not part and parcel of being a wife. Let me repeat that because it's so important: Saying "no" is part and parcel of being a mother, but it is *not* part and parcel of being a wife.

The word "no" always precipitates a fight or a conflict; and as we've learned, men hate fighting with their wives. If you were to ask the average husband what he'd like from his wife more than anything else (aside from *that*), I'd put money on his answer sounding something like this: "I want her to stop arguing with me all the time," or "I just want her to agree with me." It's not that your husband doesn't value what you think. It's that more often than not, he already knows what you think. What he wants is your approval.

Every conflict a couple faces is about two people who want to be right. But men have a particular need to be right—it's part of their manhood. They're not trying to act like children, nor is it a power trip for them. (Unless it is, but that's another conversation.) A man simply needs to feel as though he knows what he's doing at all times. If he thinks he's wrong about something, or if he doesn't have the answer, he feels inadequate—as though he's failing you. He doesn't need to be bigger or more important than you. He feels a deep sense of duty to care for you properly, and part of that means knowing what to do.

Now you might be tempted to respond with this: "So you're saying a wife is supposed to be the dutiful little woman and keep her mouth shut?" That's not it. It's okay to disagree, but only when it matters. That way when you do disagree and you discuss your points calmly and with love, your husband will listen and more than likely agree with you. When you're in fight mode all the time, he will not be responsive.

Your husband needs to know you respect him, pure and simple. And every time you argue with him, every time you say no instead of yes, you're essentially telling him you don't respect him. Besides, having someone contradict you all the time is exhausting. Imagine if every time you said black, the other person said white. Is that what your husband does to you? It's possible, but unlikely. If he does do this, he may simply be fighting fire with fire.

Try this. Try, for an entire week, to agree with your husband on every point—whether or not you do. It won't kill you, I promise. Just try it, and see how the dynamic between the two of you changes. I suspect you'll find it so pleasant it will negate your need to be right. Remember: "Being right is a dead end. Life just stops there. Nothing else happens."

You can never get someone to agree with you by telling them they're wrong. All it does is make the person feel inadequate. Even if you're right, even if you're telling your husband the truth, he doesn't want to hear it. He wants to come to that conclusion on his own.

ACTION: Stop arguing with your husband. Just. Stop. Don't say "no," or "I want to do it this way," or "I have a better idea," or some combination therein. Just trust his judgment and say, "Okay. Sounds great." The worst thing that can happen is you discover his ideas aren't so bad after all. Isn't that what you thought when you were dating him?

9

SPEAK LESS—YOU'LL SAY MORE

The second most significant proactive measure I took to improve my marriage was to stop talking so much. Pop psychology suggests communication in a marriage is everything. But in fact, too much communication can work against you. This chapter is about how important it is to be quiet. To just sit there and not say a thing.

The reason this is so important in marriage is because men are a silent bunch. They speak far less than women do—research shows women talk *some 13,000 words more per day* than men do!—not because they have nothing of value to offer but because they don't talk just to talk. They think first about what they have to say and then "bottom line" it.

That's not how you and I operate. To us, talking is second nature. And it starts when we're young. Our girlfriends come over, and we talk for hours on end, or they don't come over and we talk for hours on end on the phone. Even as adults, a "girl's night out" is filled with incessant gabbing. And if we haven't seen a friend in months and then spend two hours together, we feel like we haven't said squat. "We have to get together again," we implore. "That wasn't enough *time*."

Ring a bell? If so, that's because you're female. A man will not identify with this at all—although he will recognize it from his experience with sisters, girlfriends, and wives. Women talk. That's what we do.

I once went to a ballgame with my husband and another couple. From the moment we sat in our seats, the other wife and I turned to face each other and began talking. Halfway through the game, we were still talking—and still facing each other. The man behind us finally leaned over and asked what in the world two people could find to talk about for that long, especially in the middle of a baseball game! The truth is, we didn't even know who our home team was playing.

Now I realize that's an extreme (although 100% true) example. I'm not suggesting all women who go to baseball games would rather talk than watch the game or would be that clueless about who's playing against whom. Many women love baseball. The point isn't to demonstrate my apathy for sports—it's to demonstrate that talking is a largely female activity. And this is one area in which I'm decidedly female. If I have a thought, I need to get it out. I love to talk! To communicate! To analyze! To dissect! I could talk all day. I talk even when there's nothing to say.

> What men have mastered that women have not is the art of silence.

So, um, that was not going over well in my marriage. Men aren't wired to communicate the way women do. They communicate in a very different way, one of which involves—ironically—silence. There's a great scene in the movie *Aloha* when a military contractor named Brian (played by Bradley Cooper) is in his former girlfriend Tracy's (played by Rachel McAdams) kitchen. Tracy is married to Woody, an Air Force recruit (played by John Krasinski) who doesn't talk much. When Woody walks into the kitchen where Brian and Tracy are chatting, he looks at Brian for a really long time. Then Woody walks over to Brian, looks directly into his eyes, and then gives him a hug and walks out of the room.

Lamenting her husband's silence, Tracy says to Brian, "See what I mean?" But Brian tells Tracy she has it all wrong, that Woody spoke volumes. Then Brian tells Tracy everything he got out of the "conversation" between him and Woody, based solely on body language.

What men have mastered that women have not is the art of silence. In America, silence gets a bad rap. It's considered especially distasteful in women, who for years have been taught to speak up and to speak out. The assumption is that if they don't, they're subordinating themselves.

What bunk. Silence is very powerful.

Let's say your husband has been doing less housework than you have over the past few days. You have three options: you can demand that he do his fair share; you can ask him politely to do his fair share; or you can say nothing at all. With the first option, your husband will become belligerent in response to your demand

and conflict will ensue. With the section option, you stand a much better chance of his doing what you ask—but you'll have to be comfortable being deferential.

The third option is a win-win because it requires nothing of you, other than swallowing your pride. There will be no conflict, you won't have to muster a "pretty please," *and* you're likely to get your husband to do more chores down the road. Why? Because he will notice, after a period of time, that you've chosen to say nothing. He. Will. Notice. Men are much more responsive to nonverbal messages because they understand them so well. That's their language.

One obvious advantage to not talking so much is you become a better listener. You also have the opportunity to collect your thoughts before speaking. If Bill and I get into a particularly heated argument, he almost always disappears for a period of time. By the time he comes back, he's more focused. I never collect my thoughts—I speak them. If I don't like something, I say so. If I'm feeling frustrated or tired, I announce it. If I have an opinion, I share it. Basically, every thought and feeling I have is, or used to be, spoken.

My feelings were a faucet.

I cannot tell you how long it took me to get it and how hard it was, at first, to stop talking so much. Every time my husband would say something—whether it was about his job, or politics, our children or even a friend—I would try really really hard to zip my lip, but invariably I'd interject my thoughts or opinion. But Bill didn't want my opinion! He just wanted me to listen, which would be fine if he were just commenting on something. But if it's a problem he's having, I wanted to help solve it. To just sit there and listen and do nothing about it is one of the hardest things I've ever done. But I had to do it.

Your husband is not your girlfriend. I have a friend who, when she comes to me with a problem, actually does want my help or advice. (Same when I talk to her.) But that is not what my husband wants when he comes to me with a problem. He just wants me to sit there and listen. Because ultimately, he wants to figure it out on his own rather than be told by his wife how to handle it.

My talking wasn't just a problem in the course of conversation either. Throughout the day I would typically air every thought I had. I would also ask Bill to do things, or I would expect him to do things and let him know, either verbally or nonverbally, if he wasn't doing those things. I tried to stop, but my halfhearted attempts were hopeless, so one day I decided to go overboard. My new mantra became "Say nothing. Ask nothing. Expect nothing." I said it over and over in my head, for months, until being quiet—or quieter— became second nature.

I still have 1,000 thoughts and feelings on any given day, but now I decide which of those thoughts and feelings, if any, are worth sharing. (Hint: very few.) This is especially true when it comes to my insignificant day-to-day woes, especially ones my husband can't fix. Bill does not need to hear about everything that happens to me during the day. Discussing the minutia of daily life bogged him down with unnecessary drama he can't do anything about. Airing these insignificant woes made *me* feel better, but it made him feel awful!

So now I'm going to suggest you give it a try. Get out the duct tape and for one week, and talk only when you absolutely must. Before you open your mouth, think about why you want to say whatever it is you want to say, and then ask yourself these three questions: Is it true? Is it necessary? Is it kind? (That's a Buddhist thing.) Or you could use the mantra I did: "Say nothing. Ask nothing. Expect nothing."

The goal here isn't to turn you into a mouse. The goal is to help you take stock of your speech and to try to determine whether or not you talk more than necessary. If your goal is to be heard—and let's face it, whose isn't?—you can accomplish this using fewer words. This is true across the board, but it is especially true in your marriage.

At the beginning of this book, I said one of the things men want from their wives is companionship. Men love having a woman by their side, but not for the purpose of talking incessantly the way you and I would talk with a girlfriend. If you asked your husband what his least favorite words are that come out of your mouth, I'd bet my life savings it's, "Let's talk."

Talking is therapeutic for women. For men, it's a potential danger zone. For one thing, women are more verbal and thus take a long time getting to the point. By the time a woman gets around to her point, the man has often checked out—and then he'll get grief for having done so. In addition, talking with one's wife usually amounts to a serious discussion as opposed to some friendly banter. Many husbands find themselves in defense mode as a result.

This is in part because your husband is deeply affected by every word that comes out of your mouth. Your words have the power to lift him up or to tear him down. Once you understand this, I mean *really* understand it, it becomes surprisingly easy to pause before you speak. It may not be natural, but it will make sense once you start doing it and will thus get easier.

Your body language matters too. I remember listening to a call-in radio program and the woman told the host how unhappy she is in her marriage. But she insisted to the host that she has never *said* anything to her husband about it. To which the host responded (in jest), "Oh, you think your husband doesn't know, huh?"

A husband can read his wife like a book. He can tell by the way you *move* whether you're happy or not. And he will not easily brush off whatever negativity you exude. Conversely, he will absorb your positive nature like a sponge. There's a slight mother–son component to marriage, not in the sense that you should treat your husband like a child or even that he sees you as his mother. I mean this only as it pertains to the male wanting to please the female. It starts in childhood and never really stops. Most boys are raised by females, and then grow up to marry females. Listening to females, and wanting to please them, is in a man's blood.

So much of this book is about understanding the power you have as a female to create the marriage you want. Speaking less is part of that process. Your tendency as a female is to speak every thought you have, whereas your husband will only share what he considers important. That's why it's crucial you listen to him when he does talk. You may be tempted to tune him out, especially if you think he does the same thing to you. But if he does, it may be because you talk so much he doesn't know what's worth listening to and what's not.

Men are not poor communicators—they just get their message across in a different way. If a man has something to say, he thinks about it first to figure out precisely what he wants to communicate. Then he'll offer the bottom line and move on. If he doesn't have something to say, he's silent. This makes men naturals at business relationships more so than in personal relationships because personal relationships require more. But don't assume your husband is a bad communicator. Just learn his methods and work within that framework.

Of course, he should do the same with you—but the male-female dance demands you go first. My biggest complaint over the years is that Bill doesn't put down what he's doing and give me his full attention when I'm speaking to him. But after trying many different tactics, which all amounted to my trying to get *him* to speak *my* language, I decided to flip that around. I began to take note of how often I asked him to talk. The more I did, the less likely he was to give me his full attention. As I backed off on my attempts to communicate, I found that when I did ask Bill to talk, he was more open to listening. That's because I'm now speaking *his* language.

Here are three rules **for having a general conversation** with your husband:

1. Choose a time when he's likely to be the most receptive.
2. Bottom line it, or get to the point, right away.
3. Wait.

And here are five rules **for asking your husband to make a change** of some sort:

1. Choose a time when he's likely to be the most receptive.
2. Say something genuinely positive first.
3. Bottom line it, or get to the point, right away.
4. Be clear about what you need.
5. Wait patiently. It may take him a day or two to respond.

Men respond to sweet talk and bottom lines—not nagging, whining, and long-winded dialogue. So stop talking so much. Gather your thoughts and tell your husband what you need in two sentences or less. The fewer words you use, the more responsive he will be.

ACTION: For one week, decide to keep your feelings to yourself. Every time you want to say something, zip your lip and think first: Do I need to say this? Weigh the pros and cons before you speak. When you do speak, do so carefully and purposefully as opposed to just talking every emotion you have in order to release your frustrations. (Call or text your friend for that.) After you've been quieter than usual for a while, your husband will start to be more receptive. He'll even instigate more conversations with you. Really.

10

GET BUSY IN THE BEDROOM

There's a great scene in the movie *Annie Hall* in which a therapist asks the main character Alvy (played by Woody Allen) how often he and his girlfriend Annie (played by Diane Keaton) have sex. Alvy answers, "Hardly ever, maybe three times a week." Then the film, in a split screen, cuts to the same therapist asking Annie how often she and Alvy have sex, to which she replies, "All the time, like three times a week."[1]

The message couldn't be clearer: When it comes to sex, men and women have very different needs. These needs used to be something people understood and accepted; but in a culture that insists the sexes are "equal" as in *the same*, that understanding has vanished. As a result, so has any sympathy for men's sexual desire.

Our mothers and grandmothers understood men and had sympathy for their sexual needs. Yet another great line in *My Big Fat Greek Wedding* is when Maria tells Toula on her wedding day not to forget her "duties" as a wife. "Greek women, we may be lambs in the kitchen, but we are tigers in the bedroom."[2] Women today don't laugh at this. Instead, they become hostile—as though men can help how their bodies function. Today's culture even uses the male sex drive against men by suggesting they're prone to rape.

Men are not prone to rape. They are, however, prone to have sex.

Yes, more than you are.

I remember my mother telling me this same thing when I was much younger, and I told her she was nuts. She wasn't nuts—she was right. My favorite description of the male sex drive was explained in the book *Letters to My Daughters*, by political consultant Mary Matalin. In it, Matalin shares a funny anecdote about her mother, who once said to Mary, "Men would screw a snake if it would sit still long enough."[3] That had me in stitches!

Here's another great way to explain the difference between a man's attitude toward sex and a woman's: How many men do you know who'd be offended if a woman told him she'd like to use his body for sex? Now turn that scenario around. If a man told a woman he'd like to use her body for sex, it would be grounds for sexual harassment. Apples and oranges.

Sex is your husband's number one mode of communication—don't be put off by it just because it's different from yours. As a female, you're more emotionally expressive and nurturing and, as a result, seek intimacy via cuddling, talking, and so forth. That's not how it works for men. Men communicate via sex. Via *action*.

Your husband isn't being insulting when you walk by, and he grabs your butt. He's not being rude when he turns some innocuous statement you made into something sexual. (Lord, if I had a dollar for every time that happens in our house.) He's trying to get close to you. So let him. If he *didn't* do those things, you'd have a problem on your hands.

Of course not all men have the same sex drive. But most do, so unless you have reason to believe otherwise, you should assume your husband is like most men. Men. Love. Sex. Remember the wife store? *On the first floor are wives who love sex. On the second floor are wives who love sex and who are kind. On the third floor are wives who love sex, who are kind, and who enjoy sports.*

In the same way you and I need to talk, to *release* whatever's on our minds, men need a release of a different sort. But that release isn't just a physical act any more than your need to talk is just a physical act. When you talk to your husband and he gives you his undivided attention, that makes you feel loved, doesn't it?

It's the same way for him. Your husband wants to have sex with you because that's how *he* feels loved. And it's how he shows his love for you. If you hold this against him, or if you deny him the ability to show you his love, you're effectively telling him you don't love him. I know that's not what you mean to suggest, but that is the end result. To turn your husband down in bed is akin to telling your husband you need to talk to him about something and his saying in response, "Sorry, not interested."

Have sex with your husband regularly and often. Yes, even if you're not in the mood.

As with everything else, men take their cues about sex from their wives. If you're "into" it, your husband will almost always reciprocate. If you're not into it, he will try to get you to be more interested. But if you're not receptive, at some point he'll give up.

He's not going to force the issue forever. What's enjoyable about begging someone to have sex with you? In fact, most husbands will accept their predicament for some time. But the longer it goes on, the greater the chance he will end up in the arms of another woman. He won't necessarily seek it out. But if it's right there in front of him, and the gun is loaded…

The way to avoid this is to have sex with your husband regularly and often. Yes, even if you're not in the mood.

Now before you get your back up, stay with me. There are a few exceptions to the rule. If you've just had a baby, for instance. Or if there's been a death or a tragedy in your life. Or if you're sick or in the hospital, well, duh. But barring unusual circumstances, you need to be having sex with your husband.

If you consider this a shocking statement, you must think it's fine for your husband to not speak to you for weeks or months on end—because that's the equivalent. Think about that for a moment. Imagine your husband refused to talk to you for weeks or months. You would never stand for that in a million years!

Take Rick and Judith. Rick was unhappy with the couple's waning sex life and that unhappiness ultimately turned to anger. "She just wasn't into it," says Rick. "I understood she was exhausted, but I was hurt when she consistently turned me down. One day I decided to wait until she took the initiative. Nothing happened for five months! When I finally got fed up and asked her if she knew how long it had been since we'd last had sex, she had no clue. It wasn't even on her radar."[4]

That's not to say that over the course of a long marriage there won't be times when sex takes a back seat. That has certainly been the case in my marriage. Life with older kids was getting busier and busier, and it was hard to find time to be alone. Plus we moved to a house where the master bedroom is practically attached to our teenage daughter's bedroom. (Not a great plan, I admit; but the house worked for other reasons.) To remedy this problem, here's what I did: I flat out told my husband he wasn't initiating sex enough. Then I'd walk up to him at an opportune moment and say, "Let's have sex." Just like that—as if it were a pronouncement.

What do you think his response was? It wasn't to jump into bed. I mean, really, what's inviting about announcing that it's time to have sex? That's not exactly a turn-on. He just viewed that as one more thing he had to add to his already crowded "to-do" list: "Have sex with Suzanne."

So I decided to use a different tactic. I still waited for that opportune moment, but instead of using a "c'mon, let's get this thing over with" attitude, I put some thought into it. I'd put on something sexy or I'd flash him my hoo-ha, and what do you know? He was in the bedroom faster than a fly on a picnic table. In other words, when I shut my mouth and let my body do the talking, there he was. Ready to go.

Getting your husband "in the mood" takes two seconds, tops. It's just an entirely different experience from a husband trying to get his wife in the mood. Women need to be warmed up. We need romance and candlelight and maybe a glass of wine. Think about how much effort you both put into the act in the beginning of your relationship—it probably went on all night! Ideally, that's what women would ideally like. But once children come along it just can't happen in the same way, not on a regular basis at least. There will be far fewer opportunities to set the stage "just so."

That's called romance, and men like it too. But they're fortunate in that they don't *need* the romance in order to have sex—that's the difference. They can also tune things out more easily. Your husband can lock the bedroom door and forget about what's happening outside that door, but we women aren't like that. It's hard for women to shift from mother mode to lover mode when children are around. Each role requires a specific mindset and behavior, and it isn't easy to move seamlessly in and out of the two.

Women also have trouble disengaging from their emotions. If you and I are upset about something, it's hard to turn off those emotions and have sex. Problem is, we're saturated with thoughts. When we're flossing our teeth, we're not *just* flossing our teeth. We're flossing our teeth and thinking deeply about something at the same time. When a man flosses his teeth, he's literally just flossing his teeth.

And let's face it: those thoughts we're mulling over sometimes have to do with our husbands. We're thinking about something he is or isn't doing, or something we want him to do that he's not doing. Or we're thinking about the relationship itself. These feelings get in the way and make it hard to relax. If we don't control them, we'll be too distracted to have sex.

> Rather than wait until you're "in the mood" to have sex, use sex to put you in a better mood!

The solution to this is twofold. One, don't give your feelings so much credit (as we talked about earlier). Two, compartmentalize—the way men do. Have sex with your husband even if you're mad, sad, frustrated, or stressed out. That may sound daunting, but I will say this: it will most certainly improve your mood! Physical contact of any sort releases oxytocin, and that will make you feel closer to your husband. So rather than wait until you're in the mood to have sex, use sex to put you in a better mood! Besides, having sex will make you feel more loving, not less loving, toward your husband. It may very well eliminate whatever negative emotions you felt beforehand.

There's also this. Have you ever noticed your husband's mood immediately after sex? The change in his mood from frustrated to calm is remarkable. You could ask your husband for just about anything at that point, and he'd give it to you. (I'm not suggesting you take advantage of this fact—I'm just making a point.) It's not that different from the way you and I might feel after getting a foot rub or a full-body massage. We're like jelly, and we're far more likely to say yes than we are to say no—about anything! That's how it is for men and sex.

Sex is something that ultimately benefits both of you. When you say yes instead of no, the result is always positive. Always. Not only will you feel closer to your husband, he will be much more pleasant to be around afterward—and it lasts for days. Moreover, every sexual encounter you have with your husband doesn't need to satisfy both of you. Sometimes the two of you will be in sync; sometimes you won't. It's far better to keep having sex, and to not worry about its quality, than it is to not have sex at all.

If it's desire you're lacking, and you don't have a medical issue, it can be easy to assume you're not attracted to your husband anymore. *Don't assume this.* It's far more likely you're caught up in the daily grind, which can make it seem as though you don't feel "that way" about him.

One way to "test" it is to pack your bags and get away with your husband for the weekend. It doesn't have to be anywhere special—

just check in to your local hotel. Where you are doesn't matter. The point is to be alone without any distractions to try and get back that initial desire. Nine times out of ten, this environment will trigger the feelings you once had before life got in the way. It's amazing how quickly you can get that feeling back, which is why the more you can get away alone the better it is for your marriage.

It's also important to put the cultural messages about sex in perspective. America is saturated in sexual images and romantic narratives, which can make women think if they're not swinging from the chandelier they're somehow missing out. *Married people do not swing from the chandelier.* They can't possibly sustain that level of excitement.

That doesn't mean married sex sucks. In fact, statistically speaking, married sex is the most fulfilling sex of all. For one thing, you can literally have sex whenever you want, and it isn't fraught with angst about where the relationship is headed. Two, married couples have a shared history. Their sex isn't just about physical pleasure—it's about loyalty and commitment. That's very sexy.

All I'm saying is that it's difficult to live in a sex-saturated culture with images of uncommitted men and women getting it on all the time. If you don't ignore that influence, you run the risk of making comparisons. All of the sudden your otherwise normal sex life feels lacking, as though you're not doing it often enough or not doing it the right way. None of that is necessarily true. As long as it works for the two of you, everything's fine.

As you know, what I'm telling you is not politically correct. Women are inundated with messages that suggest a wife's needs must be met at all times before she can, or before she should be expected to, have sex with her husband. He's the one who's supposed to get her in the mood, not the other way around, by doing everything just right throughout the day so his wife feels desire for him at night.

That's not how it works.

Think back, for a moment, to the dynamic between you and your husband in the early months of your relationship. When you met, he was the alpha, and you, even if you *are* an alpha female, toned it down so he could woo you. You instinctively went into beta mode.

Your husband called *you* for the date. *He* picked *you* up and took you to the restaurant or to the movies. He paid the bill. And you took the time beforehand to dress in a certain way in order to attract him. Those things are natural because sexual attraction demands a masculine and a feminine energy. The man acts, and the woman responds.

None of that changes just because you're married. The same rules still apply. You will never be attracted to a man who doesn't take the initiative, the way your husband did back then. If your husband is not taking the initiative, it is likely because you've grabbed the reigns. You took over. You allowed your need to be in charge to suffocate his masculinity.

And he let you. *Not* because he's weak or because he's not the man you thought he was but because husbands don't like to fight with their wives. Your husband wants you happy, remember? And if being in charge makes you happy, he'll get out of your way. He will adjust his alpha level to make room for yours. That doesn't mean he's okay with it.

It means he gave up.

And I don't believe you're okay with it either. Remember the phenomenal success of *Fifty Shades of Grey*? Guess why that book hit a nerve with women all over the globe? Because sexual attraction is universal. The greatest passion you'll ever feel as a woman is when a man takes the reigns and tames you. That's what most women want, and it's definitely what the alpha female wants. It's exhausting to be in charge all the time.

Now don't run away with my reference to *Fifty Shades of Grey*. I'm not suggesting you need a red room and should hand your man a paddle. But most women do want to feel safe in the arms of someone who is stronger than they are. They want their man to be the dominant partner in the relationship, and the only reason they don't feel comfortable admitting it is because the culture won't let them. The culture wants women in charge.

But the fact is, if your sex life is lacking, or if you feel like things are "off" and you can't put your finger on why, it's likely because the dynamic in your marriage is not what it should be. If you want to get the passion back in your marriage, you need to bring back the old dynamic, the one that brought you and your husband together in the first place.

There's no way to feel amorous toward a man you've emasculated. If you've taken the power away from him—either by becoming the major breadwinner or making all the financial decisions, or by being disrespectful, or by simply becoming too alpha—the sexual energy between you has died. Think back to the early stages of your relationship. Did he make the decisions, and did you respect him? I'm guessing yes to both.

And how was your sex life?

Exactly.

The only way to revive that is to return to beta mode by putting into action all of the things you've read in this book. Those are the things that trigger passion. They demand a sexual response. Your inner beta may be dormant, but it hasn't disappeared. On the contrary, it's just sitting there for the taking.

What are you waiting for?

ACTION: For one month, say yes every time your husband initiates sex. If he doesn't initiate it, or if when you have sex it feels "off" somehow, it's probably because the dynamic you had at the beginning of your relationship has shifted. To get it back to the way it was, re-read every chapter of this book. Read it three or four times if necessary—there's a lot to take in. Only by returning to beta mode will you find what you're looking for in your marriage or relationship. It may take months or even years to recapture that dynamic. But what I've written in these pages will work. It. Will. Work.

AFTERWORD

The Alpha Female's Guide to Men and Marriage is designed to help improve both your marriage and your life, but it's mainly about shifting your paradigm. As Susan Page wrote, "If the cause of your headache is bad glasses and all you do for the problem is take aspirin, the headaches will continue to recur. You need to get new glasses."

This book represents that new pair of glasses, but it is only the beginning. To move forward, go to www.suzannevenker.com to find related resources to help you in your journey. In addition, please share your ideas, feedback and questions by emailing me at suzanne@suzannevenker.com.

And now, I have a confession to make. One of the reasons it took me so long to write this book is that I didn't want to be a hypocrite. I wanted to make sure I had done what I'm suggesting you do—become sufficiently beta—before I suggested you do the same. I mean, that's only fair, right? The truth is, I was married a long time before I got with the program. Don't let this happen to you.

I don't know how old you are, or how long you've been married, or if you even are married. But I know you have to be at a place in your marriage or relationship where you're ready to make a change, and it can take years to get to that point. But if you're able to absorb the message now, no matter where you are in your journey, all the better. You'll be that much further along than I was.

An alpha female has two options when deciding how to approach men and marriage. One is to say, "Damn it, I am who I am. Why should I change?" But alpha wives who harbor this attitude generally wind up divorced, or else they marry high beta males who let their wives rule the roost—which may work for a select few, but it won't work for most.

The other option the alpha female has is to say, "I'm not going to allow my propensity to be in charge to ruin my marriage. If I feel the need to delegate, I will satisfy that need as a mother or as a professional. But not as a wife. To love is to serve, and I choose to love my husband, not to lord over him."

So wipe the slate clean, and start today. Don't make your husband pay for whatever fears you harbor or for whatever bogus ideas the culture has taught you about men and marriage. Let him in.

DOS AND DON'TS FOR
ALPHA FEMALES

1. Hope, don't expect.
2. Ask, don't demand.
3. Praise him and thank him.
4. Say yes instead of no.
5. Let him save face.
6. Be kind.
7. Don't nag.
8. If you have to ask yourself whether or not you *should* say something, don't say anything.
9. Forget about what your husband is or isn't doing. Focus on your own actions instead.
10. Say yes to sex.

NOTES

Introduction

1. E.D. Hill, *Going Places: How America's Best and Brightest Got Started Down the Road of Life* (New York: Crown, 2009), 302.

2. *Leap Year*, 2010

Chapter 1

1. "The Roosevelts: An Intimate History," HBO. Documentary, Premiered September 2014.

2. Dale Carnegie, *How to Win Friends & Influence People* (New York: Gallery Books Reprint, 1981), 116.

Chapter 2

1. Gilbert, A. (2004, February) *Daniel Gilbert: The Surprising Science of Happiness* [video file]. http://www.ted.com/talks/dan_gilbert_asks_why_are_we_happy?language=en

2. Ibid.

3. Barry Schwartz, *The Paradox of Choice: Why More Is Less* (New York: Harper Perennial, 2005), 228.

4. Diane Sollee, Smartmarriages.com

5. Schwartz, 228.

6. Gilbert, A. (2004, February) *Daniel Gilbert: The Surprising Science of Happiness* [video file]. http://

www.ted.com/talks/dan_gilbert_asks_why_are_we_
happy?language=en

Chapter 3

1. Gabby Reece, *My Foot Is Too Big for the Glass Slipper*
(New York: Scribner, 2013),

2. Dr. Steven Rhoads, *Taking Sex Differences Seriously*
(New York: Encounter Books, 2004), 22.

3. Shawn T. Smith, *The Practical Guide to Men* (Denver,
Mesa Press, 2016), 77.

4. Dr. Emerson Eggerichs, *Love and Respect* (Nashville,
Thomas Nelson, 2004), 4.

Chapter 4

1. Terri Trespicio, "If you beat 'em, you can't join 'em."
Online video clip. YouTube. YouTube, 9 December
2012

Chapter 5

1. *Away from Her*, 2006

Chapter 7

1. Bridget Brennan, "The Top Ten Things Everyone
Should Know About Women Consumers," *Forbes*,
January 21, 2015.

2. Ralph Gardner Jr., "Alpha Women, Beta Men," *New
York Magazine*, 2011.

3. Erin Callen Montella, "Here's Ex-Lehman CFO Erin
Callan's Stunning New Memoir," *Fortune*, March 21,
2016.

4. Ralph G. Martin, "Kate Hepburn: My Life & Loves," *Ladies' Home Journal* (August 1975): 102–3.

5. "Don't Stop Believin': Everyman's Journey," HBO. Documentary, 2012.

6. Michael Noer, "Don't Marry Career Women," *Forbes*, 2006.

7. John Townsend, *What Women Want, What Men Want* (New York, Oxford University Press, 1998), 84.

Chapter 8
1. Carnegie, 168.
2. Carnegie, 145.

Chapter 10
1. *Annie Hall*, 1997.
2. *My Big Fat Greek Wedding*, 2002.
3. Mary Matalin, *Letters to My Daughters* (New York: Simon & Schuster, 2004), 45.
4. Interview, 2015

ACKNOWLEDGEMENTS

It's not easy to be married to a writer. Writing is a calling, like teaching. People do it out of passion more than anything else, and the behind-the-scenes is tough. My husband has been a saint. He's enormously supportive when I'm on a book deadline and picks up the slack like a pro. He's also as interested in and as committed to this issue as I am, which helps enormously. Finally, he's a great editor. So thank you for everything, Bill. And thank you for being the perfect combination of alpha and beta: not too strong, but never weak. You are the Best. Husband. Ever.

Second in line for appreciation is my publisher, about whom I cannot say enough. Anthony Ziccardi of Post Hill Press has made my task pure joy by leaving me to do my thing and being incredibly patient in the interim. I'd never once been late with a deadline, but this project was interrupted several times, for several reasons, and Anthony didn't flinch. Thank you, Anthony, for being so flexible and for agreeing to publish whatever book I ended up giving you. I hope its quality is what you'd hoped.

READING GROUP QUESTIONS

1. Are you an alpha wife? If so, have you always known it even if it didn't have a name?

2. Are any of your friends or family members alpha wives?

3. How does your personality compare to your husband's? Are the two of you generally compatible?

4. Which part of the book resonated most? Which parts did you not agree with?

5. Do you agree with the author that the alpha wife should "tone it down" at home? If not, why not?

6. How has your view of power changed as a result of reading this book?

7. Do you know any beta wives? If so, what is the dynamic in their marriages?

8. Do you know any marriages that have ended or are mired in conflict as a result of the wife being too strong?

AN INTERVIEW WITH THE AUTHOR

The Alpha Female's Guide to Men and Marriage *is certainly controversial, but it's also personal. Was it difficult to write?*

Very much so. In fact, I came close to abandoning the entire thing on more than one occasion. I might have done so if my mother hadn't died in the middle of my writing it.

I think that was one of the things that was holding me back. I wanted so much to do right in using her marriage to my father as an example of what *not* to do, so obviously I wasn't sure how she'd receive it. After she died, I felt freer to write the book. But it was important to me that I honored both her and my father, for whom I have great respect.

The other reason I struggled to complete the book has to do with what I wrote in the afterword: I was still trying to become a better wife myself through the process, and I didn't feel I had it down until several months before I finished the manuscript. I knew what was happening in my marriage, but I wanted it to be either a done deal or to be at least fully in process before the book was published.

In the book you explain that, like any personality trait, there's a "spectrum" when it comes to being an alpha or a beta—also known as 'type A' and 'type B.' Where do you fall on the spectrum?

I'm a High Alpha/Mid Beta, which means I'm dominant in most relationships but "have the capacity to collaborate and compromise." I do, however, have to "guard against imposing my strong will" and thus overpowering others. My results also say I match up well with a partner who's more laid back than I and can help me take the edge off.

Fortunately, I married someone with that profile. (The second time anyway; my first husband and I were both high alphas.) My husband's score landed him the "High Beta/Mid Alpha" range, which means he's a "good mixture of Alpha and Beta." He is "confident without being overbearing." He is "cooperative" but often prefers to let others lead but he's not a "pushover" because he can "hold his own."

So on paper this looks like an ideal match—and it is—but that doesn't mean life is smooth sailing. Like everyone else, we have to figure out the right balance for us because my alpha-like nature invariably collides with his.

As far as the spectrum goes, I'm probably a 7 or 8 in my professional life. But at home, I've learned to tone it down, so I'm more of a 4 or a 5.

I was never rude or disrespectful toward my husband in the past, nor did I make demands on him (well, I might have tried; but he'd always reject my efforts), but what I did do was just as exasperating: I wouldn't let up. I'd carry on with something until I got my way, and he'd eventually relent because the conflict wasn't worth it.

I was just always in fight mode. I had to have the last word, or I had to correct something if I knew it was wrong, or I had to "direct his traffic," as he would say. And at the end of the day, I didn't want that kind of relationship anymore. I didn't like the way it felt, and I didn't want the arguments that would inevitably go along with it. And I *know* he didn't.

It sounds like, from what you wrote in the book, that you're an alpha female because the women in your family were alphas and you absorbed that. Can you speak to this?

I do come from a long line of alpha females, that's true. But I actually had a double whammy in that my father was a major micromanager! Micromanaging is something alpha females are prone to anyway, so that influence certainly didn't help my case. While my mother modeled a take-charge attitude, my father was constantly micromanaging everything. Looking back, it was probably his way of asserting control.

Look, all of us are born with certain personality traits, but what we experience growing up has a huge effect as well. My parents were great people who passed on hugely—hugely!—positive traits, for which I'm eternally grateful. But like everyone else, they were human. They also lived at a time when people didn't talk about the whys of human behavior, and neither one of them was self-reflective. As a result, my parents ended up having the same arguments over and over. I don't think this is unusual for couples in a long marriage; I just personally didn't want to live that way. It's exhausting.

What, or who, is an alpha female? And is the message in your book that women shouldn't be alphas anymore?

An alpha female is a leader. As a wife, you may find the alpha female at the office or you may find her at home with the kids. How she spends her days doesn't matter—what matters is how she behaves. An alpha wife takes charge of everything and everyone. She is, in a word, The Boss.

This attitude/personality trait/approach to life—whatever you want to call it—can work well in the marketplace or even as a parent. But as a wife, it's a disaster. No man wants a boss, or even a competitor, at home. That type of relationship may work for a spell, but it will eventually come crashing down.

So the answer to your second question is: yes and no. It's fine to be an alpha in certain areas of life, but love requires masculinity and femininity if it's going to run smoothly. One leads; the other follows. One makes the first move; the other responds. One drives the car; the other sits in the passenger seat. This means that when an alpha female marries your average guy, she's going to have to channel her inner beta if she wants a peaceful marriage.

Do you think marriage, or the relationship between the sexes in general, is more difficult than it used to be? If so, why?

I don't think many people would look at the past and say things were perfect, but there was definitely a time when gender relations weren't fraught with so much tension, anger and resentment. There was a healthy respect for gendered preferences, too, which is so important. To accept human nature, to flow with the tide rather than against it, is just smart. It's one thing to encourage the sexes to think outside the box as far as gender roles go—people have to be flexible—and another thing to suggest biology is bogus and that the goal should be an "equal" marriage.

Playing tit for tat is a recipe for failure. Marriage is a partnership. As long as both partners are thinking "we" instead of "me," they're in good shape.

I also think the Internet, while a boon in so many ways, has had a negative effect on relationships. In addition to pulling couples away from each another, we become privy to what everyone else is doing, or what it *looks* like everyone else is doing. Women are particularly susceptible to this. They make comparisons, which is toxic. Marriage is just so much easier without those negative influences.

What do see as the future of the marriage?

I'm very concerned. Since 1970, the divorce rate has quadrupled; and it has happened at the exact time women have become the more dominant sex. Is it a coincidence that 70% to 80% of divorce is now initiated by wives? I don't think so. I think women don't know *how* to be wives. And why would they? That isn't what they were taught to become.

Modern women have been raised to rule the world, not to get married and have kids. They're also products of divorce. How could circumstances like these possibly result in strong marriages?

The good news is that any woman can master the art of wifedom by understanding this one concept: The skills you need to pursue a career, *or even to raise children*, are the exact same skills that will destroy your marriage. If you want to get married and stay married, you need a whole new set of skills.

That's the reason for *The Alpha Female's Guide to Men and Marriage.*